Sea Urchin

Sea Urchin

A CHILDHOOD AT SEA

Christina Rees

N

North River Press
Croton-on-Hudson, New York

Library of Congress Cataloging-in-Publication Data

Rees, Christina, 1953-
    Sea urchin : a childhood afloat / Christina Rees.
      p. cm.
      ISBN 0-88427-079-3 : $17.50
    1. Rees, Christina, 1953- --Childhood and youth. 2. Rees,
Christina, 1953- --Journeys. 3. Seafaring life. 4. United
States--Biography. I. Title.
CT275.R356A3 1989
910.4'5--dc20
[B]   89-37930
                                  CIP

Manufactured in the United States of America

North River Press
P.O. Box 309
Croton-On-Hudson, NY 10520

To my Parents With Love and Gratitude

I would like to thank Maike Herlyn and Danielle Koninkx for their much appreciated practical support during the writing of this book. Above all, I am deeply grateful to my husband Chris for his painstaking and time-consuming technical assistance, and also for his steady encouragement, all of which enabled my words to become a proper manuscript.

Contents

Sea Urchin

Foreword

On the 14th of October, 1958, a bright yellow schooner sailed out of Northport Harbor on Long Island. On board were three small children, their parents, and a cat. As they sailed away, they waved at a quayside rimmed with people who waved back at them. The children did not know it then, but they were also waving goodbye to life as they knew it.

I was five when my parents sold our home, gave away our dog, and took me, my sister Robin, who was seven, and my brother Joel, who was four, out for a sail that was to last over seven years, with only brief sojourns back into a conventional life style. As far as we children were concerned, we were just going out for a long sail, an extended holiday. My parents were more aware of just what we were doing, but even they could not have foreseen the adventures that lay ahead.

They realized that they had much to lose, but if things went well, they also had much to gain. At forty-two, my father had left his job with Oxford University Press, work that had taken him around many of the university campuses in America looking for professors who were working on special projects that could be turned into books. My mother, who was thirty-seven, had stopped teaching years earlier, even before Robin was born. With this trip, they stepped out of the traditional working world, and Daddy left a career that he was never to take up again. My parents sold our house, our sweet white wooden house that was so cozy and comfortable, with its tidy garden on its nice treelined street. They sold our car and left our friends, neighbors, and family.

I was unaware of it at the time, but some of our friends and relatives tried to talk Mommy and Daddy out of going. They painted the worst possible picture of what might happen, the blackest scenario of life on a boat with three small children. Looking back, I wonder if my parents' decision may have threatened many of their friends. What some of these people might have been saying to Mommy and Daddy was, "Don't go and take this risk, because I could never take the risk. Your going is making me face the fact that I may talk about it, but I would never have the courage to do it."

Socially, it was difficult as well. We know how to relate to people if we can see their cars or sip tea with them in their houses and speak to them about their jobs, but how do we relate to people who have discarded all points of reference, who have abandoned the set criteria used to determine exactly who they are and where they fit in society? Where does sailing through life on a small wooden schooner fit in? Our proposed life style confounded many people, even the ones who wished us well.

Perhaps now our life style would raise fewer eyebrows; perhaps if we had set out even ten years later than we did, our leaving would have made more sense to more people. But in 1958, it was not the vogue to be different, to do your own thing. During our travels we would occasionally meet other families who were living on boats, and each would have a story to tell. But sailing families were rare. It was much more common to meet sailing couples, two people pledged to each other and to their lives afloat. We even met some boats more than once. Our paths would cross in unlikely places, and when this happened it was like meeting old friends. Those of us who lived on the sea shared a strong bond. Whether or not we even knew or liked each other, we all wished each other calm seas and fair winds.

In thinking of how to write about our time aboard the *Tappan Zee*, I realized that I could not remember all the details in perfect chronological order. Exact dates and places are lost to me, if indeed I ever knew them. For much of our early travels, I was just too young to be concerned with the hard facts and figures of getting from one place to another. I retain innumerable disconnected memories of the past, isolated faces and places, tastes, sounds, sights, scents, and feelings which I can recall with great clarity but which I cannot fit into the overall picture. However, shining among these fragments like nuggets in a pan of gold dust are vivid memories of complete events. I have chosen to write the stories of these events. I see this book more as a collection of short stories than as a continuous, unfolding tale. There is, of course, much that I have had to leave out, but I believe I have drawn together the core of our adventures. I now invite you to step aboard the *Tappan Zee* and come out for a sail. The weather looks promising, and we have all the time in the world.

Christina Rees
Barley
July 1, 1989

CHAPTER ONE

Watermelons and Low Tide

The day of our departure dawned cool and gray. It was October 14, 1958. We were filled with excitement and could not wait to set off. Mommy and Daddy must have been frantic and nervous as well as excited, but they did not show it. They let us children help with the last-minute packing, which by now consisted only of food and a few pieces of clothing. I do not remember leaving our house for the last time or saying goodbye to our dog, a black and white cocker spaniel named Telemachus. We did not have to say goodbye to our cat, Tipsy, because we had decided to take her with us. We had not planned to, but a few weeks earlier we had gone to our boat, which was then moored off shore. We piled into the dinghy for Daddy to row us out, leaving Tipsy and Telemachus on the beach. We had not got very far when we turned back to see both animals swimming out to us, their little worried faces held out of the water. Knowing how cats hate water, we were impressed by this costly demonstration of affection. My parents decided that we would take Tipsy, but even with all the love in the world, a small schooner, especially in rolling seas, is no place for a dog.

Over the last few weeks and days, I suppose our friends and neighbors must have come to say farewell, but I recall nothing of it, only a sense of looking forward to the future. I felt as if we were beginning a holiday that would never end.

On the day we set off, we arrived at the quay where the *Tappan Zee* was tied up and waiting. She looked like a plump beast of burden being loaded before the start of a journey. Happy and frisky, she tugged impatiently at her ropes.

Daddy had bought the *Tappan Zee* in 1946. She was rigged as a schooner, with two masts, both fifty-two feet tall. They were raked slightly toward the stern, which gave her a particularly graceful line. The foremast was positioned right at the front or bow of the boat. At the foot of the foremast, the anchors rested on the deck. The mainmast rose out of the middle of the boat, and attached to that, at about five feet off the deck, was the boom. The boom stretched back from the mainmast and out over the end or stern of the boat. The bottom of the mainsail was attached to the top of the boom. The boom could swing free, and depending on the wind, was either kept fastened close in or allowed to swing way out to the side. I was too short to hit my head on the boom, but

Mommy and Daddy always had to duck when crossing from one side of the boat to the other.

The *Tappan Zee* was painted a deep, rich, golden yellow with green and white trim. The decks were white, as were the masts. Each of the masts was made out of a single tapering tree, sanded until it was smooth. On the left side of the boat we hung a red oil lamp, indicating that it was the port side; on the right we hung a green lamp, indicating the starboard side. At the bow and stern were white lamps.

The *Tappan Zee* was built to a Dutch design used on Block Island, a small island near Long Island off the east coast of America. The design had been used for fishing boats and for ocean sailing boats. We have met a sister ship, a boat made around the same time to the identical design. The sides of the *Tappan Zee* rose out of the water and swelled to make the boat look plump, if a boat can look plump. She was steered by a large rudder at the stern connected to an eight-foot-long, varnished wooden tiller.

A tiller is a long piece of wood or metal that is connected to the rudder at the stern of a boat. We had a tiller instead of a steering wheel. If we wanted to turn to the right, it was necessary to push the tiller to the left, and vice versa. Robin was ambidextrous, but slightly more left-handed. There were many times when Daddy would shout a steering command, and she would push the tiller in the wrong direction. It was a family joke that Robin got confused between right and left, but it was a gentle family joke, because we all made the same mistake--even if we did not do it with such predictable regularity.

Both the bow and stern of the boat came to a point. This type of design is known as a double-ended boat. She sat in the water rather like a large, floating American football, sliced in half the long way, with two tall poles sticking up out of her. I grew to love the *Tappan Zee* and felt passionately loyal to her, even when sleeker modern yachts would pull up alongside and make her look rustic and rotund by comparison. She was known as a "character yacht," which I think suits the *Tappan Zee's* long and varied life.

Because the *Tappan Zee* was made entirely of wood, she always needed upkeep. This upkeep included scraping, preparing, sanding, varnishing or painting the wood. The sides or hull needed recaulking from time to time to keep them watertight. We painted the bottom of the boat with seaweed-resistant paint, but still the seaweed grew. Since having seaweed on the bottom can slow a boat down, we would have to dive overboard frequently with large, stiff scrubbing brushes and scrub her bottom.

Overall, the *Tappan Zee* measured thirty-eight feet in length by fourteen feet in width at the widest place. The bowsprit, the piece of wood which protrudes from the bow, added another six feet or so. This may seem large to someone accustomed to rowboats, but for a family of five, with all the sail bags and other gear, it was a tight squeeze. Our engine was an Ailsa Craig, thirty-five horsepower diesel engine. It was huge and sat in the middle of the boat between my bunk and Robin's, its wires and caps and valves exposed like a prickly metal monster. There were parts of it that got hot and parts which had to be kept smeared with grease, so we had to be careful not to fall onto it. Also it made a tremendous noise, but it did not take us long to become accustomed to that. There was something soothing and soporific about its roar. It was so loud that we had to shout to be heard over it. We soon learned how to sleep through the sound of the engine--as well as the shouting!

Forward of the middle two bunks where Robin and I slept were two more bunks, angled into the bow. Joel slept on one, and the other was used for storing sails, except when we had a guest. Mommy and Daddy slept in the main cabin. There were no doors in the boat, and their area was divided from ours by a curtain and a row of hanging clothing. The toilet or "john" was pinched between the two bow bunks. Later this was moved to the middle section, but for years we had to make our way forward and squeeze into the tiny triangular space, smaller than a telephone booth, between the bunks.

Being an old-fashioned boat, *Tappan Zee* had no running water. The toilet was flushed by depressing a foot pedal while pulling a hand lever back and forth until the toilet was clear. This could take several minutes, and when we first started the trip, Joel could barely reach the pedals! As you can imagine, there was little privacy. We had to dress, undress, and wash in front of each other. There was simply no option. My parents must have perfected the art of other activities in total silence. But of course, at the time, we children were oblivious.

We became accustomed to nudity and in the warm weather wore nothing but a pair of shorts. Sometimes when we swam from the boat we would strip them off and jump overboard without a stitch on. We kept clean with a daily splash on our hands and faces and often with a swim. When the boat was tied up to a dock, we would shower each other with a hose, which was a luxury. Also we had a large plastic tub for the washing, and we would sometimes fill that and sit in it. That was the closest we got to a proper bath. We washed our hair once a week or once every two weeks, more or less, when Mommy insisted. I remember that we used Breck

Shampoo, which used to sting my eyes, but it always left my hair feeling light and silky, which was a delicious feeling after days of salty swimming.

The sink, being the only one, had to be used for all our washing needs, from cleaning grimy hands to preparing food. One such occasion, when Robin was brushing her teeth while Mommy was trying to make some sandwiches, spawned what became a classic and oft repeated line in our family, "Don't spit on the lettuce!" The sink was in the main cabin and also had to be pumped. Fresh water was a precious commodity aboard the boat and we used only what was essential. Our main supply was a seventy-gallon tank, and for long sails we would take extra water.

Across from the sink was our stove. It was a two-burner Sterno stove and it swang on gimbals. That allowed us to cook even in rough weather, although usually we did not eat in rough weather. But it also helped during the times when another boat would go by and cause us to rock. Next to the two burners was a potbellied wood-burning fireplace. This was our only form of heating, and there were many times when we were glad of it.

All the imperishable food was stored under Mommy's bunk behind wooden slatted doors. Behind the stairs leading up to the deck, we had an icebox. Whenever possible we kept a huge chunk of ice in it and put the food on top of that. We used only powdered milk and very little butter. We had to eat tinned food when we were sailing, but we could usually catch fresh fish for protein. When Mommy was able to shop on shore, we would stock up on fresh fruit and vegetables, but when we ran out, that was it. No popping down to the local shop and no going out to a restaurant for a quick snack. This life style has left me with a deep appreciation for dinners out, showers, baths, refrigerators, flush toilets, electricity, and hot and cold running water. The boat was home, and home was good, but now I realize what its limitations were as well.

It was essential that everything have a place and be returned to it after use. There was simply no leeway for mess or leaving things about. When we accumulated too much for the spaces available, either we would have to give or throw something away, or, if it was valuable and could be used in the future, send it to be stored at my father's parents' home on Long Island. Usually we gave things away. We discovered in the sailing community that books are passed around from one boat to another. We were always being given countless paperbacks, which we then gave to someone else when we had finished reading them.

But all of this lay ahead of us as we loaded on the last of our provisions at the dock in Northport Harbor. The tide was low, and it was a long jump down from the side of the quay to our deck. Robin and Joel and I had to be handed down by someone into Daddy's arms. There was a crowd of people on the quay side, staring down at our boat, and watching us as we prepared to cast off. There were words from well-wishers, a hug, someone wiping a tear, lots of laughter, and many kindly and curious eyes.

As a going-away present someone had given us ten large watermelons. Joel was struggling to hand them down to Daddy. He could barely lift the melons, but he so wanted to help. One of the onlookers, a midget, came over to Joel and offered to help him. The man bent down and put his arms around a melon and then stood up again to hand it over to my father. He, too, could barely hold the melon, it was so large and his arms were so short, but, like Joel, he was determined to help and become a part of our leaving.

The melons were at last loaded and the last bits of our gear tucked into place below decks. Besides our immediate family, my father's elder sister, Olga, was to accompany us for the first leg of the journey. We all loved our Aunt Olga, whom we called "Ogi." She was an artist and lived in New York City and had often sailed with us on shorter trips. Mommy and Daddy said their final good-byes to their friends and hopped onto the boat. Daddy started the engine, which immediately drowned out all the farewells being called to us. Someone on the shore cast us off. The adventure had begun. We were beginning a new life, one that would replace our old routines, one that would now define our terms of reference. We children were too young to have thought about this or to understand the implications of the step that our parents had taken.

Years later, in school, I studied a poem that has since then been with me. Somehow it has stood as an explanation for the times when I have felt in need of one. That poem is Robert Frost's "The Road Not Taken."

The Road Not Taken

Two roads diverged in a yellow wood
And sorry I could not travel both
And be one traveller, long I stood
And looked down one as far as I could
To where it bent in the undergrowth;

Then took the other, as just as fair,

And having perhaps the better claim,
Because it was grassy and wanted wear;
Though as for that, the passing there
Had worn them really about the same,

And both that morning equally lay
In leaves no step had trodden black.
Oh, I kept the first for another day!
Yet knowing how way leads on to way,
I doubted if I should ever come back.

I shall be telling this with a sigh
Somewhere ages and ages hence:
Two roads diverged in a wood, and I--
I took the one less travelled by,
And that has made all the difference.

Our move onto the boat was a decision made by my parents, for them and for their children. It changed their lives, but because Robin and Joel and I were so young, it did something more than change our lives. It formed them. For my parents, it has become a time in their lives, one time among others, a time set in a larger context. For me and my brother and sister, it has become the context too. I often feel that new friends cannot really begin to understand me until I tell them, "I grew up on a boat."

CHAPTER TWO

Down the Intracoastal Waterway

We set off down the Intracoastal Waterway. That was to be our road for the next four months. The Intracoastal Waterway is a series of canals and bodies of water that runs roughly parallel to the east coast of the United States from New York to Florida. The waterway is protected from the Atlantic Ocean at times by broad sections of land and at times by mere clumps of floating grasses or sand banks. It is an ideal route for smaller boats and boats that are not made for ocean travel.

Daddy had bought all the charts we needed to get us from Long Island down to Florida. We sailed down the East River until we left Manhattan and the more built-up areas of New Jersey and came into wilder sections of the waterway. In 1958, much of it was untouched and wildlife was abundant. We saw bald eagles and other birds of prey. We sailed silently by grazing deer. We spotted wild turkeys bustling through the undergrowth. One day a deer plunged into the water right in front of us and swam across the canal, its nostrils held above the water, its eyes wild with fright. Because we traveled so slowly, the equivalent of about four or five miles an hour, we saw everything in great detail. The water and the shore line provided a continually unfolding tapestry of delight. We had an excellent pair of binoculars that could even be used at night. If any of us saw something moving in the distance, we would look through the binoculars hoping to discover a rare sight. Sometimes we could all see a dark spot of something moving or floating, and we would bet on what it was. "It's a deer," one of us would cry out, or "It's a blue heron." "No it's an osprey," and then out would come the binoculars, and we would find out the truth. Sometimes the truth was no more than an old wooden stump worn into an interesting animal-like shape. Then we would tease the person who had first alerted the rest of us to the shape.

We became very good at spotting fish as well. That takes a special type of concentration. An animal or bird usually stands out from its surroundings. Also, its movements help to identify it. Spotting fish, however, requires one to stare into the water, ready to detect the slightest variation in shade or the tiniest movement underneath the surface. If a fish is decent enough to jump out of the water and show itself off, then the task is much easier. But it was possible to spot resting fish and fish lying motionless in a shadow or slipping swiftly by the boat. Often the glare of the sun on the water prevented us seeing all that we could have. Overcast days, even though we preferred the sun, were actually better for spotting fish.

We fished, we ate, we anchored off shore, or sometimes we would pull up alongside a dock to let Tipsy have a run on solid ground. She was not entirely at home on board and sometimes would yowl pitifully. She fell overboard once or twice and absolutely hated that. However, it was not till we got to Atlantic Highlands, about one hundred miles into the journey, that she decided she had had enough. She jumped ship one night and the next morning she was nowhere to be seen. We tried calling her and we asked local people to watch out for her, but no cat. We stayed at the dock for a few more days hoping to see her, but finally we had to move on. It was obvious that Tipsy had made up her mind and had chosen dry land.

Robin and Joel and I were devastated, but we realized that she had made a choice. Mommy and Daddy told us nice stories of how she had gone ashore because she had met a cat friend who had asked her to stay. That made us feel better. None of us wanted to think of Tipsy roaming the streets of Atlantic Highlands growing thinner and thinner, having to protect herself from street-hardened alley cats and stray dogs. That was the first unhappy experience we had with a pet. Many more were to follow.

Mommy had been trained as a schoolteacher, so we children were encouraged to study. We had books to read, and we did spelling and simple arithmetic. Mommy and Daddy told us stories from history, and we had nature all around us for the sciences. As part of our lives we studied biology, zoology, and botany, as well as astronomy, meteorology, geography, palaeontology, oceanography, conchology, and ornithology!

And, of course, we received daily instruction in practical skills. We learned to sand a rough bit of wood until it felt like a smooth stone. We painted, at first the things that were easy, like large sections of the deck. This was laid with canvas which was stretched tight and painted white. Later we were given small brushes and shown how to varnish thin strips of railing. We polished the bell, the rims of the portholes, the compass, and any other piece of brass that needed polishing. We were taught to coil ropes, to tie them, and to make them fast to cleats. After a while it became second nature. We helped to pull up the sails and lower them. We learned to row with the large wooden oars that we used in our bright yellow, molded fiberglass dinghy.

We also learned how to catch fish with a fishing pole as well as with a drop line. I would fasten a small bit of bait, usually some leftover meat from our last meal, and perch as motionless as possible by the railing of the boat. Then I would gently lower the line, and sit with it curled over my index finger, holding the remainder of it in my other hand. Whenever there was a nibble, I could feel it tugging on my index finger. Depending on the strength of the tug, I would respond with a little jerk of my finger or stay motionless and wait for a more substantial bite. I found catching fish to be a great thrill, one of which I never tired. There was something exciting about feeling the line pulling away from me, knowing I had hooked a fish. Sometimes we caught catfish, which we threw back, sometimes we caught flounder, which were very tasty, and sometimes we got the many other types of small fish that inhabited the waterways. Occasionally we would hook something larger and much heavier, but it usually broke the line before we could land it. We had numerous experiences with the one that got away--all true!

Our daily chores were to make our bunks upon rising, fold our night clothes and put them away, and then help Mommy with breakfast, if there was anything we could do, or if not, just stay out of the way. Later we helped Mommy and Daddy with their turns at the helm. We would sit in the cockpit with them, feeling very grown up. In time, we were allowed to adjust the lines if the wind was not too strong. We learned to throw out the anchor and read the currents; we learned about trimming the sails according to the direction of the winds. It was a life totally involved with nature. We were dependent upon the tides, the depth of the water, the winds and the general weather conditions. If the water was choppy (that is, light waves that throw up a bit of spray and disturb the surface of the water) we knew that we would be in for a bumpy ride, and we knew that it would be more difficult to catch fish. Fish do not like to bite when it is choppy nor when it is too windy. They prefer a nice calm day, and they have feeding times during which they are much more likely to bite.

I remember when I first tried to clean a fish. It seemed impossibly slimy and slippery, and I could not even hold it, much less scale it. At first Daddy or Mommy would kill the fish for me and then let me struggle clumsily as I scraped off the scales. Later I progressed to killing, gutting, and filleting the fish, something that I learned to do within minutes.

I loved fish. I loved to eat them. But mainly I loved to watch them underwater and see their bright colors flashing and their graceful movements. I can remember wishing that I could breathe under water so that I could swim around with the fish. I think I would have liked to have been a cross between Dr. Dolittle and a mermaid--the best of both worlds.

We made our way slowly down the waterway, gliding silently by old wrecks of boats, dilapidated shacks, crumbling docks, and miles and miles of untouched swamp and canals. At certain points we needed to go through locks. As the locks would fill up with water, we would rise higher and higher or sink lower until we could move on. Once as we waited in a lock in a stretch called Dismal Swamp Canal, the lock keeper sold us a large jar of pine honey, with the comb in it as well. I loved the honey and I loved to chew the comb. At other times we had to go under bridges. Some of the bridges were too low for our masts. Daddy would have to study the chart, and if the height of the next bridge was less than 55 feet, he would take out an odd-looking horn that he cranked with a handle and make several blasts on it until the bridge keeper was roused to shut the bridge to traffic and open it to us. The horn made a loud "AOOGA!" noise. "AA-OOO-GA, AA-OOO-GA!" It usually fetched the bridge keeper straight away, and then he, or she, would pop back into the control tower and start the mechanics to open the bridge.

Most of the bridges opened from the middle, just like a huge gate swinging open, only upward instead of on its side. Sometimes the bridge keeper would send down a message. To make sure that it landed on our deck instead of floating into the water, the message would be fastened to a small sandbag. We would all have to take cover so that the sandbag would not hit us on the head. One time, Daddy shouted, "Sandbag!" and we scattered to safe places. This time I could not make up my mind where to hide. Our dinghy was on the right-hand side of the deck upside down. Finally I decided to hide under the dinghy, but I was too late. I had just squeezed my head and shoulders under the small boat when "plomp," the sandbag landed right on my upturned bottom. Everybody found it hilarious but me. I pulled my legs and backside under the dinghy and stayed there for a long time, nursing a slightly sore bottom and an even more seriously wounded pride.

I was not a clumsy child, in fact I was very agile and dexterous, but I seemed to have the habit of getting in the way. I liked to be close to my parents and close to what was happening, and sometimes that was in the line of action. "Oh, Christina," my mother would say in an exasperated voice, "you're in the way again." My father, being a man of fewer words, would just shout again." My father, being a man of fewer words, would just shout "Gangway!" and then I would try to dive out of his way. In my own defense, I was not the only one who got in the way; we all got in each other's way--it was impossible not to. But I suppose I did have a special talent in this area.

When I was not getting in people's way or catching supper, I was playing with my alphabets. I kept my bag of alphabets in a small brown-paper bag. The alphabet was made of colored plastic letters which could be attached together. I loved those letters, and I would make up words endlessly, snapping and unsnapping the letters. For a time I carried the bag around with me all day long, and I can remember feeling somehow whole and complete with my letters--have alphabet will travel. I also had a pair of sunglasses. We all had to wear sunglasses. It would have been uncomfortable and unhealthy to have to squint all day long, in the glare of the sun on the deck and on the water. My pair of sunglasses had pinkish rims with gold speckles in them and the glass was tinted green. They made me feel suave and confident. With my bright orange bulbous life jacket, my cool shades, and my bag of alphabets, my daily outfit was complete.

Not far into the trip my parents got a brilliant idea. They hoisted up the dinghy between the two masts until it was about ten feet above the deck. Once secured, it made a perfect crow's-nest and playhouse. My father would lift us in, one by one, and we would sit up there quite happily for hours on end. The view was much improved from up in the dinghy, and often we spotted birds and animals that my parents could not see. This arrangement made the *Tappan Zee* look a bit strange, but it was perfect for us, a nautical equivalent to a playpen.

At other times the sun burned down so fiercely that we put an awning over the mainmast boom which was over the tiller. Thus, the person steering the boat and anyone else under the awning could sail in cool shade while the rest of the boat sweltered in the heat.

Below deck there was little that could be done to vary our living space, but we three children went through the stage when we wanted to have our bunks curtained off. So our ever-willing Mommy patiently strung up some unused sheets across the openings to our bunks to create secret hideaways. In time, of course, we grew tired of being curtained off from each other, but it was great fun for a while.

We played chess and checkers and hide-and-go-seek. It seemed impossible to hide on our boat, but we could and did. Joel was so incredible at folding himself into the tiniest of spaces that he fooled all of us. He could curl up underneath a sail or squeeze behind a mattress or even crouch down in the bottom of a tiny cupboard, where with a bit of camouflage he was undetectable. Perhaps his prize hiding place was in the shallow food cupboards under Mommy's bed. He could squeeze up on top of the various tins of food and flatten himself against the inside of the hull so that no one could see him, not even when looking into the cupboards.

The two obvious places to hide were the bow and the stern. At the bow the sails were stored in great, heavy, lumpy canvas bags. It was easy to slither between two sail bags and disappear from view. In the stern we had the seventy-gallon tank of fresh drinking water. Behind that was loose storage space where we kept our skin-diving gear, our flag and flagpole, and other pieces of equipment. I could slide from Mommy's bunk, past the bilge pump handle, past the water tank into the dark, cool, and slightly scary no man's land of the aft storage space. In a way, hiding there was not fair; even if someone was positive that I was there, it was impossible to be sure without going in after me. It was just too dark and big and full of provisions to be able to distinguish a hiding child.

With our chores and fishing and tending the ropes, the days passed happily. They were full, but they were not frantic. Robin, Joel, and I spent hours each day drawing. Mommy had procured a large end of a bolt of newsprint from a local Huntington newspaper before we had left. Daddy hung it on a pole, and we could pull down and then cut off as much or as little of the paper as we liked. We all drew furiously, producing quantities of masterpieces which we would proudly present to our parents. Quite incredibly, Mommy bothered to save some of this "early" work which still survives today!

There was no phone and no television, just a radio that Daddy controlled. As I remember, it played the most brilliant static. For years on end I listened to static and snatches of song that would phase in and out and sometimes get overtaken by a news report in a foreign language. There were times when I would quite happily have thrown that radio overboard! Our only lighting was from a few oil lamps. They were beautiful. The ones in the main cabin, where we ate and where Mommy and Daddy slept, were on gimbals suspended from the wall, able to swing freely with the roll of the boat and yet stay upright. The lamps were brass, with graceful, curving, open-ended glass hoods which fit into brass prongs around the base of the wick. Over the lamps we had umbrella-like brass shields screwed into the wall to prevent the smoke from discoloring or scorching the ceiling. After a day of sailing or gentle motoring, we would throw out one or two anchors and descend into the cabin where Mommy would have lit the lamps and the Primus stove. The sun-baked day would disappear over the horizon and become a soft dark star-twinkling night, with our little lamps glowing with warmth and coziness. Every night Daddy would hang out the port and starboard lamps, red for port (left) and green for starboard (right), so that we could be seen by a passing boat. We would bob and rock gently, the rigging slapping lazily in the breeze and a rope squeaking from time to time, with only the occasional sound of a fish jumping, either pursuing or being pursued.

Except when we were too hot, or it was too bitterly cold, we never had trouble getting to sleep. With the boat rocking and with the peace of the evenings, sometimes we were so sleepy that we would fall asleep at supper. Then Mommy or Daddy would scoop us up gently and deposit us on our bunks where our shoes would be pulled off and our covers pulled up and a last kiss planted on our foreheads. All night the boat would rock us, and the small waves lapping at the side would sing a soporific chorus. Those were the good nights.

There were bad nights as well, when the wind would come up and a storm would blow and we would be miserable. The gentle rocking would turn to pitching and wild swaying, and everything that was not screwed down would shake and rattle and roll. Instead of being lulled to sleep, we would be kept awake by the jerking movement of the boat and the howling and lashing of the rigging. And if those nights were also cold, we would go to bed with layers of clothes on, shivering and damp. There is a dark side to living on a boat and of living so close to nature, so dependent on the weather. At those times it seemed to me as if the world had become my enemy, ugly, angry, and dangerous. All our laughter, our carefree happiness seemed to be mocked in a storm. It was as if the world outside our little cabin was saying, "Friends? I never knew you."

When a storm would finally die, it was as if we could all breathe again. We could stop fighting to survive and get on with living. The morning after a storm Mommy would hang the damp bedding over the boom and prop the sodden cushions up on their sides to dry. Daddy would test the anchor rope to see if and how much we had dragged, so that the next time he would know how to anchor us better.

Robin and Joel and I would be set the simpler chores of tidying our shelves and clearing anything else that had rolled out of place. Sometimes we would find a small fish on our deck, one that had been whipped up from the water in the storm, or a dead bird that had been blown off course.

As we sailed further south we began to see some of the deserted plantations that had been the centers of power of the old colonial estates. Huge mansions that once had been filled with the privileged white families who owned vast cotton fields and hundreds of slaves now stood like bleached skeletons on the sides of the waterway. Some were in ruins, but those nearly whole stared at us as we ghosted past, the windows like dark and cavernous eyes, lost in generations of thought, relics of a time gone by. Even the grand old trees drooped mournfully, dripping with long gray beards of Spanish moss, strangled by vines and creepers. The houses looked so sad, as if their memories of gaiety and grandeur had sentenced them to a barely living hell. We sailed quietly and solemnly past this strange graveyard, history weeping at us from the weed-choked shores.

It was then nearly Christmas, and we had crossed from Georgia into Florida, the last state going southward down the east coast of America. Robin and Joel and I were very excited and tried to figure out how Santa Claus would come down our chimney. We decided that he could not possibly fit down the small smokestack which led up from our potbellied stove and we knew he would have to choose a different route. We decided that he would just have to come down the cabin stairs like everyone else.

We pulled into a small harbor up the New River in the heart of Fort Lauderdale. Twinkling lights hung on the palm trees that lined the river. It was only a few days before Christmas, and Mommy and Daddy hoped they could find some presents for us. They were almost out of cash and had no idea what to get us. Mommy was privately worried that we would not have a happy Christmas, but she revealed none of this to us. We children were just thrilled with the thought of Christmas, and we had complete faith in Santa Claus' ability to find us.

The day before Christmas, when we were all below, we suddenly heard a voice calling our names. We shot up out of the cabin, to find Granddaddy and Grandmother! Mommy's parents had driven all the way from California to be with us that first Christmas. They had received Mommy's last letter to them saying where we were. Then they had figured out how far we would have gotten and drove to the likely area. Once at the waterway they asked if anyone had seen a yellow sailboat with a family aboard go by. As we were hard to miss, people had seen us, and my grandparents managed to track us down without much difficulty.

I did not know this at the time, but their coming saved our

Christmas. Besides the love and fun they brought to us, they also brought presents. Their trip east to find us was a brave labor of love and generosity, and Mommy in particular was thrilled to see them. All I knew at the time was that Granddaddy and Grandmother were with us and everything was all right.

On Christmas morning, we woke up early and raced into the main cabin. There on the floor was a pile of presents! Grandmother gave dolls to Robin and me, and she had made the most beautiful clothes to go with them. Granddaddy had made little wooden wardrobes that fastened shut with a brass pin. Our gifts from Mommy and Daddy were a hula-hoop apiece. We scrambled onto the shore and practiced making the hoops stay up on our hips. We laughed at each other and hula-hooped for hours on end. Later Mommy told me that they were the only presents she could find in the town and that they had cost about fifty cents each! But they were precious to us and we treasured them.

Granddaddy and Grandmother stayed with us for about two weeks, and then they left to make the long drive back to California. Mommy wept, and we all felt miserable saying good-bye to them. They were wonderful and loving, but what bothered me most was seeing Mommy sad.

We continued southward to Dania, a small town nestled up one of the innumerable side canals that made up a network of waterways just inland from the vast expanse of the Atlantic Ocean. We moored at the marina, which was little more than a few docks surrounded by mangrove swamps. We soon learned that these watery woods were the home of, among other creatures, a colony of mangy monkeys who had escaped from a traveling circus. The monkeys had adapted fairly well to their new home, even though they probably had to work much harder to survive in their free state than they would have had to in captivity.

Dania was quiet, totally private, and very different from the more civilized waterways of Florida. There were no houses here, no clipped hibiscus shrubs and thick manicured lawns with shiny boats bobbing contentedly at the ends of private docks. Instead we had escaped monkeys, wild racoon and opossum, all the wading birds, land crabs, as well as the fish and the manatees.

Manatees are huge air-breathing creatures that look like somewhat bulbous and comical seals, with large round bodies and dumpling fat cheeks. I adored the gentle manatees which we would spot from our boat, slowly munching their way through floating fields of water hyacinths. Every so often a sweet whiskery face would rise out of the water and take a breath before submerging again. I remember longing to make friends with these shy creatures, wishing that I could swim with them and ride on their backs as they rolled lazily down the canals. Even though we were often visited by the manatees, for some reason it was always a special treat to see them.

We needed to stop and dry out for a while, and Mommy and Daddy had decided that we children should go to school, so Daddy found a job as a salesman and decorating consultant for Castro Convertibles furniture shop. The owner had offered us the use of his empty property and dock in nearby Boca Raton. No doubt he was intrigued with his new employee's somewhat unusual living conditions!

So, we left Dania and putt-putted to Boca Raton which was to become our new home for nearly two years.

CHAPTER THREE

Boca Raton

We found ourselves tied up to a large dock on a beautiful lake also called Boca Raton. We were the only boat at the dock. It had one outlet for water and one for electricity. Our view across the bay was of a huge hotel, the once splendid Boca Raton Club.

At that time the Boca Raton Club was in shabby condition. It had been designed in a grand Spanish style for an era that had passed. Now it is booming again, but when we lived on the lake, the hotel had a dilapidated air about it. The most wonderful and startling thing about the club was that it was painted bright pink. I loved to gaze at it across the bay and wonder how many rooms there were and what they looked like. For me it was a place of magic and fantasy.

The lake was large and there were houses dotted around the shores, most of them tucked away behind palm trees, bougainvillea bushes, and other exotic greenery. There were a few docks at which motor boats were moored, but near us there was nothing. It felt as if we were the only people living on the lake.

Next to our dock was a small vacant lot where we children could play. The lot was full of pricker grass, a grass about a foot tall with stalks branching out with tiny seeds, each protected by a covering of spikes. The prickles were like miniature horse chestnuts, only much sharper. We were constantly stepping on them and yowling and pulling them out, only to step on another batch of them minutes later. They became part of life in Boca Raton. There were also hibiscus bushes with flame-red blossoms that attracted hummingbirds, so it was not all bad.

Across the road stretched miles of sandy beach and beyond that the Atlantic Ocean. The beach was almost always deserted, as no one lived near us. And so we found ourselves on what amounted to a private lake, with our own private ocean front across the road. The sails were folded and stuffed back into their bags and the *Tappan Zee* was tied fast to the dock. We had found a new home.

Robin entered third grade at the local school. I had turned six, so I started first grade. Joel went to nursery school or stayed with Mommy. We bought a car, and Daddy started thinking about rigging the boat for electricity. We were becoming rather civilized.

After school and on the weekends we crossed the road and splashed into the ocean. We had been doing this for a few months when my parents bought us each a mask, snorkel, and flippers. We could not wait to use them and raced across to the beach, pulled on the gear, and jumped in. Seconds later we shot out of the water, screaming with fright. We had been surrounded by a school of barracudas, not large barracudas, but barracudas nonetheless. As we lay panting on the sand, whimpering with fright, a thought came to my mother: Just suppose that the barracudas had been swimming with us all along? Suppose they were quite happy with us? After all, it was we who had flapped out of the water. The fish had not acted frightened of us, and usually it is the other way around.

Mommy has always been brave, with a fearlessness and pioneering spirit that would shame lesser mortals. Years later, when I read about Joan of Arc, I recognized my mother in that noble martyr. That day on the beach Mommy strode back into the water to test her theory. We children huddled at the water's edge, hoping and praying that Mommy would not be attacked right before our eyes. Happily, she was not. She swam about calmly, her head in the water, mask and snorkel in place. When she surfaced there was a broad grin on her face. "It's all right!" she called out. "They're fine!" We pulled back on our flippers and masks and hesitantly swam out to her. The barracudas were still there, but they kept a constant distance of about three feet between us and them. If we swam toward them they would swim away from us, and if we swam away from them, they would follow at the set distance.

It took a while before we trusted the barracudas, if one can call it trust. Barracudas are sleek silver and black predators, fast and evil looking, with rows of jagged, needle-sharp teeth. A full grown barracuda can measure over six feet, but these junior barracudas were only about a foot or two long. I cannot really say that they became our friends, but we did become comfortable around them, and we continued to share their stretch of sea by the beach.

We did make friends with some of the other fish. There was one particular type of fish, only about an inch long, which loved to swim by our masks and dart in front of our faces. It would stay with us the entire time we were in the water and only abandon us when we got too near the shore.

We practiced holding our breaths and diving down to the bottom. In a very short time we became good skin divers. Robin and Joel and I used to throw heavy shells or stones for each other and chase each other and play tag. We frolicked like a family of porpoises in our newly discovered undersea world.

Meanwhile, life on land was progressing nicely. I had a lovely teacher named Miss Rose Cormier, who looked like a young Queen Elizabeth II. She liked me, and I became an enthusiastic student, listening hard so that I could answer all her questions. Our class was a mixture. There was Patty Ann Shea, sweet and sensible, but never a prig; she was my best friend. There was the blond and freckled Barbara Ham, who was my second-best friend. And there was one girl who was from a poor family. She would come to school with unwashed and uncombed hair, her clothes filthy and torn. Sometimes she came with bare feet.

One day she came to school without any underpants on and was discovered by some of the other children who immediately started teasing her. Miss Cormier stepped in and asked the girl where her pants were. The poor child said she did not have any pants on because she did not have any to wear. I don't know what Miss Cormier did, but the girl always came to school with underpants after that. I felt sorry for her, but she was painfully shy and did not mix easily.

It was in first grade that I first fell in love. He was a handsome boy with bright eyes, a dimply smile, and a fashionable crew cut. His name was Michael Key. I was mad about him. During play time I would chase him and try to pin him down so that I could kiss him. He struggled, sometimes hard, sometimes not so hard. For the hard times I recruited Patty Ann to help me wrestle him to the ground. Once we had him down and pinned, we would take turns kissing him, while he would wriggle and scream and shout, "Yuck!" But I could tell he loved us too, and we were blissfully happy.

Back on the *Tappan Zee* Daddy was making headway with wiring the boat for electricity. He would drill holes here and there and shove wires down the walls of the cabin and then try to hide it all as best he could. During this time we made trips up to New York to see Daddy's parents and we went to see Mommy's parents in California. Mommy and Daddy were a case of East meets West; for all the interests and love they shared, they were opposites in many ways.

Mommy was a mixture of five bloods: English, Irish, French, Dutch, and German-Swiss. Her ancestors had come to America in at least two shifts. One group crossed the plains in covered wagons and went all the way to California. Another group settled in some of the eastern states. Family history has it that as her western ancestors were bumping along in their covered wagons, they were intercepted by the fearsome Indian chief Cochise. Of course, everyone in the wagon train assumed that they were going to be killed. Instead, Cochise ordered them to stop and started looking them over. Then he spotted my great-great-grandmother, who was at that time just a babe in arms. He went over to her mother and demanded to hold the baby. Very gently, Cochise showed her around to his people. Great-great-grandmother had flaming red hair, and it appeared that Cochise had never seen red hair before. When Cochise had finished showing her off, he handed her back to her mother, and the wagon train was allowed to carry on, unharmed. So the story goes.

Most of Mommy's family stayed in California, but some went on to Hawaii. One of her great-great-aunts married Philip Rice, who became the first Chief Justice of Hawaii. The Rice family still lives in Hawaii, and Mommy and her brothers and sister have visited them several times. However, most of the family settled in California and scattered up and down the coast where they still live today. Mommy's father was a cattle rancher as was his father before him, and Mommy's mother, when she wasn't providing food for a house full of cowboys, feeding the chickens, drying the venison, making clothes, or tending the gardens and orchards, was an artist.

By all accounts, one had to have a goodly portion of true grit to survive that life style. Mommy was brought up in the saddle, and everyone was expected to know how to ride and shoot. Mountain lions, bobcats, coyotes, and rattlesnakes were frequent visitors, and guns were an everyday part of life. If one avoided the snakes and wild cats, there were always the scorpions, tarantulas, and other dangerous insects. For my mother's family, hunting deer was not a sport; venison was a staple of their diet. I remember seeing pairs and pairs of antlers in Granddaddy and Grandmother's home. Even when we visited their ranch in 1960, we had to step around rattlesnakes a few times out on walks. Also, Mommy crushed a tarantula with a rake after one had tried to take a nap with Robin. Along with the tarantulas there were tarantula wasps, wasps which would fight tarantulas, and then if successful, lay their eggs in the tarantulas' dead bodies. Those wasps were like flying commandos and frightened me almost as much as the tarantulas did.

It was definitely not a life for the squeamish or delicate, and it was clearly a perfect preparation for Mommy's married life afloat. As well as being an expert horsewoman, Mommy was an excellent archer, swimmer, violinist, and dancer--plus she had acquired her commercial pilot's license. Her greatest loves were nature and people, and she became a teacher when she left college. During the Second World War she spent several happy years in the cockpits of various Cessna aircraft. She had even worked in aircraft maintenance and repair.

In addition to all this was her physical appearance. Mommy stood over five feet seven inches tall, slender, with broad shoulders; she had immaculate posture, high cheek bones, piercing, warm brown eyes, and dark brown hair. When her skin turned dark olive in the sun, she closely resembled everyone's idea of an Apache Indian. In fact, when Daddy brought her home to meet his parents, his father was convinced that Mommy was an Indian. Later, after their marriage was announced in the *New York Times*, complete with photograph, Daddy's father received a letter from a man with an Indian name claiming to be one of Mommy's relatives. He asked for a large loan and promised that he would repay it soon. Grandpapa was conned and wrote out a hefty check which he gave to the man. Of course, money and man were never heard of again. Grandpapa never quite believed that Mommy was not part Indian, and Mommy could never believe that Grandpapa had fallen for the trap. She, like most Americans, would be proud to have Indian blood. What bothered her was that her own father-in-law had believed a crafty con man and had not believed her!

So this athletic creature left the sagebrush and mountains and traveled three thousand miles east to team up with my father. Daddy had three different nationalities in him: Russian, German, and Swedish. His father was an architect, tall and charming, but a fierce authoritarian to his family. Daddy's mother was a diminutive Russian, a sculptress. Except for her strong and muscular works of art, everything about her was delicate, refined, exquisite. Daddy grew up with five languages being spoken in his home, which was in Flushing, Long Island, not far from New York City. He sailed, rowed, went out and about in New York City, and spent his summers in the Hamptons, a group of villages further out on Long Island.

Like his parents, Daddy could draw beautifully. But he did not want to become an architect just like his father, and he did not have the single-minded commitment to art to take after his mother. He loved opera and the theatre and books. After university he joined Oxford University Press. During the war he was in the United States Air Force and flew ninety-nine missions as a radar observer in Black Widow night-fighter planes. But his overriding passion, ever since he had been a small boy, was boats. Daddy built them, sailed them, made models of them, and even before he had met my mother, he had already bought the *Tappan Zee*.

Physically, Daddy and Mommy could not have been less alike. Daddy was about the same height as Mommy, strong and agile with well-rounded muscles. He had pale blonde hair and sea-blue eyes. Is it any wonder, then, that at times sparks would fly between them or that their progeny should at times feel such strong cross currents within themselves?

While the rest of us were still visiting Mommy's parents in California, Daddy returned to the *Tappan Zee*. The idea was that Daddy would complete the electrical wiring of the boat, so that when we rejoined him a week later, we would come home to a boat that could be lit with the flick of a switch. Daddy installed lights throughout the boat, and for the first time we experienced the luxury of reading in bed. We would still have to use the oil lamps when sailing, but, from then on, whenever we were tied up to a dock with an electrical outlet, we could plug in. It was a new type of freedom and Daddy was a hero.

At about this time I saw my father suffer one of the several bad injuries he had while we lived on the boat. One such accident was a severe blow to his temple from the metal handle of our anchor-rope winch. It failed to latch on one of the ratchets and unwound at speed when Daddy was standing right next to it. This time, however, he was injured by a fish.

One of us children had caught a catfish, and we wanted to unhook it and throw it back into the water. Catfish are slippery, scaleless creatures with fleshy whiskers sprouting from either side of their mouths, which give them their name. There are numerous varieties of catfish. Some are equipped with dorsal fins (the fins on the top of their backs) which become erect when the fish is frightened. The first spike of the dorsal fin on some catfish is a poisonous barb which the fish can release into an enemy.

This time the enemy was Daddy trying to get the fish off the hook. It wriggled and struggled in Daddy's hand. Daddy's grip slipped, and the dorsal fin shot up, the barb stabbing into the palm of Daddy's left hand. He dropped the fish, screaming with pain. The barb was buried deep in his palm. It had sunk so deep that he could not get a grip on it. He hunched up with pain and made horrible sounds as he tried to pull out the barb. The three of us children could only look on with wide eyes, completely helpless, whimpering at his pain. Mommy tried to pull out the barb, but with no success. It just made Daddy scream the more with pain. "Get the pliers!" Daddy shouted, "Get the pliers!" Mommy scrambled down to the tool box and re-emerged with a pair of pliers.

Daddy was sweating and shaking and groaning all at once, but he grabbed the pliers from Mommy with his good right hand and gripped them around the barely protruding stub of the barb. With an almighty tug and twist Daddy pulled out the barb. Blood poured out of his hand and dripped down his arm onto the deck. By this time Robin, Joel, and I were all crying loudly. Mommy got a rag and wrapped it around his hand, and then she bustled him and us into the car. We drove to the doctor's with Daddy slumped in the front seat, moaning and shaking.

Mommy took Daddy in to see the doctor. About half an hour later he came out with his hand wrapped in a white bandage, but he was smiling weakly. He was going to be all right. We children had been told a million times never to try to unhook a catfish if we caught one. Having seen what Daddy had gone through, we never had to be told again. For a long time I remember hating all catfish. Just the sight of one would make me want to kill it. But our memories healed, and Daddy's hand healed--even though he had the scar for a long time.

Christmas came, as Christmases do, even to Florida. Instead of looking forward to snow and sledding and sitting around a crackling fire, we had only our holiday decorations to make it feel like Christmas. We bought a small tree and hung shells and baubles on it. Elsewhere in Boca Raton people put plastic Santas on their roofs and plastic reindeer prancing across their lawns, along with the pink plaster flamingos and the real bird-of-paradise flowers and the real great white and blue herons that wandered in and out of everyone's gardens. It was an odd and incongruous mixture, but it helped to make us believe that Christmas really was at hand.

Mommy has the mixed blessing of having her birthday fall on Christmas Day. Although no one forgets a Christmas birthday, there is often only one present a year to do for both occasions. Mommy used to tell us how upset she would get as a child when beaming relatives would hand her just one present and say, "Happy Birthday and Merry Christmas, Carol!" As far as she was concerned, that was cheating.

For our second Christmas in Florida, we children plotted and planned what to give our parents. For Mommy we came up with the brilliant idea of giving her a bra. Why a bra, I have no idea, but a bra it was. Obviously, we had to tell her so that she could drive us and herself to the shops to find one. I believe she was rather touched with our thoughtfulness, and it was true that the elastic in her bras was getting old. Leaving Daddy behind, no doubt tittering to himself, we set off on our bra-hunting expedition. One might have thought, through ignorance or one's own fortuitousness in similar matters, that it would be a simple task to buy a bra. For us it was not.

Mommy took us to a large department store in Fort Lauderdale where there was bound to be a sumptuous choice of ladies' undergarments. Mommy strode bravely into the store, flanked by us three children offering our considered opinions as to which type and style of bra we should buy. We wove our way through the jungle of clothes racks and smiling mannequins until at last we came to the more hushed and rarefied area of ladies' lingerie. A determinedly gracious saleslady approached our merry band and inquired if she could be of any assistance. Robin and Joel and I drew ourselves up and Robin spoke. "We want to buy a bra for Mommy." "For her birthday," Joel offered, bright eyed. "And for Christmas," I added, bushy tailed. Barely a flick of the eyelids and the lady altered her tactics. "Of course," she said calmly, "and what would you like to see?" There was an enthusiastic babble during which words like "lacy," "big," "round," "soft," and "pointy" could be heard. "Yes, yes," our lady murmured, "I see."

She turned and swept over to a counter filled with trays of bras. "And what size would that be?" she asked over her shoulder. Mommy pronounced some numbers and a letter that meant nothing to us, but made us feel that things were progressing swimmingly. The lady placed several delicate items on the counter top for our inspection. We picked them up and felt them and prodded them. This was the era of padded bras, and we were being shown particularly fine examples of the style. Some had cups which stuck out in points, others were more rounded but no less reinforced. Each of us grabbed a bra that we felt Mommy would love. "This one, Mommy," we all cried, pressing the bras upon her, sticking our fingers and fists into the cups. Mommy grinned down at us and looked over the bras.

"Perhaps Madam should try them on," the saleslady purred, beginning to get into the spirit of our quest. Clutching the bras we trotted behind the lady over to the curtained-off changing cubicles. Mommy dutifully slipped off her blouse and her own bra and began trying on the bras we were eagerly holding out to her. Each bra was greeted with "Oooo"s and "Aaaah"s and surveyed critically by the three of us. We insisted upon pressing it and poking it to get the feel of it. We favored the ones that could stand up on their own and which sprang back into shape after being poked with a finger.

We were oblivious at the time, but Mommy despised anything that was false or unnatural. Because of our enthusiasm the saleslady assumed that Mommy was happy with the styles being shown. She came in with another arm load of bras, in an assortment of colors, each one more lavishly reinforced than the last. Patiently and graciously Mommy tried on each bra. Some were too tight, some too big, and others just did not feel right. Robin and Joel and I were completely engrossed in finding the perfect bra. We swarmed over Mommy, adjusting, stroking, and endlessly patting her bosoms as if to reassure them that they were going to be well taken care of.

After a lengthy session of trying on, Mommy sat in the small dressing room surrounded by a heap of discarded bras. None of them was right. Mommy did not have a new bra. A gloom was beginning to settle over us. The saleslady deftly exited and reappeared almost instantly with another bra. "I think you'll like this one," she said with a wink at my Mommy. And then, before our very eyes, she proceeded to blow up the cups of the bra. It was their latest style, inflatable cups for a little extra oomph. Joel was sold on it immediately. With wide eyes he poked the bra. "Oh yes, Mommy, yes, please get this one!" The kind lady showed him how he could blow up the balloons in the cups for mother. Joel was entranced. The saleslady pointed out to Mommy that she did not always have to use the inflated cups. She could take them out or put them in as she wished. It seemed to us children too good to be true. Mommy had only one course of action--she had to buy that bra. Mommy tried it on and then handed it to the saleslady. "We'll take this one." she said, nobly. Christmas was going to happen after all!

We could not wait to get home to show Daddy, and bounced up and down in the car with excitement. "Do you like it, Mommy?" we asked, "Do you like it?" Mommy committed perjury and swore that she loved the bra. We were blissfully happy.

Mommy had managed to keep a straight face during the entire shopping expedition, but when she had to model the bra for Daddy, the edifice crumbled. Daddy took one look at the elaborate inflated lacy superstructure protruding from Mommy's chest and collapsed with mirth. The bra gave Mommy a completely different silhouette. It looked as if she would knock things over with her new enlarged bosoms every time she turned around in our small cabin. Mommy stuck out her chest and paraded in front of us while Daddy shook with laughter and wiped the tears from his eyes. Mommy began to laugh too, a laugh that had been bottled up for hours. Soon we were all laughing, even though Robin and Joel and I did not quite know what was so funny. All we knew was that Mommy and Daddy were happy and that we had bought Mommy a new bra. It made us feel very proud. Mommy rarely wore the bra with the pads inflated, but Joel had hours of fun blowing up, then squishing, then again blowing up the small cushions.

At this time, but quite independently, Daddy had purchased a pair of leopard-spotted panties for Mommy. They had just come into the market, and Daddy must have bought one of the earliest models produced. Like the blow-up bra, they were not exactly Mommy's style, but they were made so well that she was stuck with them for years!

One warm and lazy day I was playing in the vacant lot beside the boat. I had on only a pair of red panties. All along the waistline I had stuck in large, red hibiscus blossoms. I also put a blossom behind both ears and one between my toes. The flowers made me feel special and beautiful, and I pranced around the lot, skipping over the sharp prickers and frolicking among the hibiscus bushes and in and out of our tent. Daddy had erected a makeshift tent for us in the vacant lot. It was nothing more than a tarpaulin slung over some poles, but it was wonderful, a place where exciting things could happen.

In the middle of my carefree, flower-bedecked fantasy, Joel came bounding from the cabin. "Grandmama's dead!" he shouted, "Grandmama's dead, and you are supposed to come downstairs." We always called the interior of our boat the "downstairs," even though that is not the proper nautical term.

I stopped my dancing and looked at Joel. He sounded as if he were telling the truth, but sometimes you couldn't tell with Joel. This time it had to be a lie.

I turned my back on him and sang out, "You're lying. Go away." But Joel just hopped up and down and became more insistent. "No, no, it's true. It's true. Daddy got a letter and he's crying."

I felt this joke was going too far. First of all, grandparents don't die, and second, Daddy never cried, except for things like the catfish barb. I felt Joel's joke was in bad taste. "I don't believe you," I sneered and ran away from him.

Joel looked confused and upset, then he ran back onto the boat. Two seconds later my mother's head poked up out of the cabin. "Christina," she called, "can you come here please." I froze in my tracks. Her voice had a control and an authority--even though it was a kindly authority--in it that I had never heard before. So Joel . . . I could not imagine it. Grandmama dead? But how? And how awful of me not to believe him. I went running onto the boat, pulling out the hibiscus blossoms as I went, my play world suddenly out of place, embarrassing.

I shot down the cabin stairs to find Robin and Joel huddled around Daddy who was sitting down, his blue eyes bright aquamarine and streaming with tears. Robin and Joel were weeping and sniffling. An opened telegram lay on the table. I didn't want this to be true. I didn't want any of it to be true, not Grandmama dead and not my father crying.

"Grandmama has died, darling," Mommy said to me in a soft and soothing voice. I did not want her voice to be soft and soothing. I did not want any of this to be true. Grandmama couldn't die! She was . . . GRANDMAMA! I burst into tears and joined the huddle around Daddy. Our sobs mingled and poured out of us. We cried together until our weeping turned to hiccupping and until our eyes could not cry any more. And then we all blew our noses and slowly, hesitantly, started talking.

Grandmama was the first grandparent--indeed, the first close relative--to die. I loved her deeply. I loved her sweet voice with her soft accent, the way she would cock her head to one side and grin impishly at us. She was like an exquisite bird, trapped in a cage of arthritis and in her wheelchair. She made us wonderful clothes, smocked beautiful dresses, and created magical puppets, all with her bent and gnarled hands. I never thought about how awful that must have been for her, confined to a wheelchair and crippled with arthritis, no longer able to sculpt her magnificent statues. All that mattered to me was that Grandmama was there and that she loved me. She was always cheerful, always interested, delighted, surprised, always there. Only now she would not be there any more, not for me or anyone. Whatever would Grandpapa do? What would he do without Grandmama?

Daddy flew up to Long Island for the funeral. I was confused and worried about what might happen. Would Daddy change? Would he be always sad from then on? But when Daddy came home again he was his normal self, just a little quieter, and even his quietness did not last for long.

Grandmama died when she was seventy-three, severely crippled with arthritis. When younger, she had been a brilliant sculptress and painter. As a young woman she had lived and worked in Paris. Even the great Rodin had seen her work. He had been brought to her studio to critique her art. Evidently, when he saw her sculptures he had immediately pronounced that they could not have been done by a woman. Then, after studying them for a while, he had said, "There is nothing I can tell you." And then he left! The statues she had been working on then were nudes, large and muscular, like some of Rodin's own statues. He could not believe that a petite and delicate young Russian girl could have modeled such statues.

While in Paris she also took piano lessons from Madame Rimsky-Korsakov, the wife of the famous composer. And it was in Paris that she first met my grandfather.

Grandpapa had been in Paris en route back from Turkey, where he had been commissioned to design a library for Robert College in Istanbul, then Constantinople. I have no idea how long he spent there, but he used to tell us endless stories of his adventures. He must have had a knack of getting involved with mischief, possibly even initiating it, because there were many wild stories. One was of a lady who somehow ended up in Grandpapa's room, whom he had to talk out of stabbing her husband with an enormous butcher's knife. Then there was the story of taking a donkey upstairs in a large expensive hotel. Grandpapa had been shot at in Constantinople for rowing a boat too near a Turkish harem where he was enjoying a close-up look at the women, so he had jumped into the Bosphorus and swum for his life. In addition to all this, he got cholera and nearly died.

We grew up with these and many more stories and with the lovely songs he used to sing while playing his beautiful zither. The zither is a bit like a small harp in a box which is rested on the lap to play. It had a most warm and vibrant tone, and I could listen to Grandpapa play it for hours on end.

But always there was Grandmama. She had begun to be crippled with arthritis when she was about forty-five and soon had to give up her art. When her children started producing grandchildren, she began to make puppets and to smock dresses and shirt fronts, but it was a far cry from doing what her hands once had been able to do.

There were four children, of whom Daddy was the second. They all had nicknames. Olga, the eldest, became "Ogi"; Daddy, John, was "Cundy," from *secundus* (Latin for the second). Daddy's younger brother, Peter Paul, was "Doody," and his younger sister, Eudoxia, was "Doxie." Grandmama herself was "Minky," and Grandpapa was simply "Papa."

When visiting Bridgehampton, Robin and Joel and I used to play a horrible joke on Grandpapa. In the mornings Grandpapa would make coffee in the kitchen, which was quite a distance from his and Grandmama's bedroom. The three of us would sneak into their bedroom, help Grandmama into her wheelchair, and make their bed. Then we would go tearing to the kitchen, shouting, "Grandmama's fallen out of bed!"

The first time we did it, Grandpapa dropped what he was holding, and with a look of terror in his eyes, ran into the bedroom, only to find Grandmama sitting primly in her wheelchair beside the wrinkle-free bed.

I think he could have strangled us, but he just laughed, relieved. After that first time, we played that joke every morning while we were visiting them. It became a ritual, and Grandpapa would always drop whatever he was doing in the kitchen (usually he was in the process of tossing one of his enormous German pancakes), and with a look of horror on his face speed to the bedroom, pretending to be so surprised to see Grandmama sitting up and the bed made. Robin and Joel and I never tired of the ritual, and we always half believed that Grandpapa really was frightened every morning. Grandpapa was later to die of a heart attack, and I suppose we should be thankful he did not die the first time we played that joke on him.

Our grandparents' house was full of treasures. Besides the statues, which sometimes frightened me, there were smaller carvings of graceful nudes and many small *objets d'art:* an ivory puzzle that was a series of carved balls, each intact and each inside the other; a large wooden egg, as large as an ostrich egg, that opened to reveal smaller eggs inside with a tiny chick no bigger than a peppercorn in the very center--and then there was The Box. The Box was an ivory and ebony inlaid box the size of a large tea chest. The front consisted of two doors which swung open. Behind them was another series of doors and drawers. If certain drawers were taken out, and a wall extracted, a hidden row of three drawers would be revealed. Grandpapa always kept a fake diamond ring in one of the hidden drawers and pretended to find it for the first time every time we saw it. We would beg him to open the chest, and after acting as if he did not want to, finally he would agree and the magic would begin.

Their home was a large wooden-shingled house built in 1814. It had five fireplaces, one of which was in the bedroom Robin and I stayed in, which much, much later was to become my own bedroom. There was a maid's room over the kitchen, with a doorway opening onto the steps which led up to the room. Cut into this door was a cat hole, a round hole with a panel of wood over it which could be clawed back if the cat wanted to get through. That cat door delighted us, and we would play for hours on the old stairway, shouting to each other through the hole.

The house was a place of mystery and magic with all its art, as well as its huge attic full of dusty treasures, and an equally huge basement, musty and festooned with cobwebs. Outdoors was also a place of wonder. The garden was large and full of wonderful trees: lilac, spruce, chestnut, holly, apple, and crab apple. There were bushes of old roses, smoke bushes, rows of privet, clumps of rushes, beds of lily of the valley and bluebells, an herb garden, a grape trellis over the entry way, and a highly productive vegetable garden. But best of all was the grand old beech tree.

The beech tree had been brought over on a ship called the *Louis Philippe* in 1843, along with many other trees and seedlings for the colonists living on Long Island. However, the ship was wrecked off the shores of Long Island, where much of its cargo floated ashore. Some of the roses and English beech trees were in pots which were washed ashore and then rescued by the local farmers, who planted them in their gardens. My grandparents had one of the rose bushes and one of the beech trees. The beech tree was towering in height, with thick branches that drooped gracefully above the ground. Riding these branches was as much fun as riding a horse. We would shimmy up onto the tops of the branches and rock up and down for hours. Sometimes Mommy or Daddy or Grandpapa would come out and rock us, sending us even higher.

Our visits with Grandmama and Grandpapa were always wonderful. Now with Grandmama dead, I did not know what to expect. I thought about the next time we would stay with Grandpapa. For me, I knew that the house would always be filled with the presence of Grandmama. She would be there, invisible, watching over us and all our doings, silent and loving, but somehow sad that she could not join in. Sad and wise. I felt she would know exactly what to do at all times, now that she was dead.

Sometime after Grandmama died, Mommy and Daddy told us that we were going to move. Because of a new job for Daddy, we were going to sail to a group of islands called the Bahamas where we could swim and fish and collect shells to our hearts' delight. This sounded excellent, and we said goodbye to Boca Raton and our friends with relative ease. I had to drop out of the Brownies before I had earned my first badge, but Brown Owl, being an understanding woman, gave me a little golden star and said that she knew I would have made a good Brownie if I had stayed.

Mommy and Daddy were very busy, stocking the larders, filling up with fuel and water, making sure the sails were in good order. We would have to go back to using the oil lamps and no longer would we have easy access to fresh water.

The day of our departure came, and we disconnected ourselves from the electricity outlet and cast off from the dock. We motored happily out of Boca Raton Lake, staring back for a last look at the big pink hotel. We were on the move again.

CHAPTER FOUR

Crossing the Gulf Stream

The voyage from the east coast of Florida to Grand Bahama Island is seventy miles across open sea. Part of that open sea is the Gulf Stream, a current of warmer water that flows from the Caribbean up the east coast of Florida and then northeast across the Atlantic to the west coast of Great Britain.

It was to be the longest continuous sail we had done as a family. My mother had stocked the cupboards with tins and tins of Dinty Moore stew, asparagus, corn, corned beef, plum tomatoes, fruit juices, and other staples. She had brought in more Saltine crackers and Carnation powdered milk, cereals, porridge oats, and jars of peanut butter and jam.

We hoped to arrive in the Bahamas in two days. On the first day the sea was a sparkling deep blue, the wind steady, and we scooted happily away from our homeland, little realizing that it would be four years before we returned to live on American soil. During the days we fished, drew sketches with pencils and crayons, and helped out as the official crew of the *Tappan Zee*.

Daddy was Captain; his word was law. Mommy was First Mate. As the crew, we children had certain duties. We coiled ropes, and we could trim the sails and steer. We could already row the dinghy and read the compass and perform many other of the day-to-day jobs of a sailor.

One of our duties, which we took turns doing, was washing the dishes. As our water tank held just seventy gallons of water, we had to be extremely careful only to use the fresh water when absolutely necessary. This early conditioning has stayed with me, and still I cannot bear to hear the sound of tap water running if it is not being used. (I also still consider baths to be a luxury--even though I do take one from time to time!). So, to save our drinking water, we would dip a bucket overboard, haul it up, and wash the dishes in the clean ocean water.

On the second day of our crossing to the Bahamas, we were sailing across the Gulf Steam. The water was brilliantly clear and sparkling. Mommy was so inspired by its crystal-like purity that she decided to conserve the drinking water and make the breakfast porridge with sea water. "After all," she mused, "I always salt the water anyway, so why not use water that is already salted?" It seemed like an excellent idea. All of us except Mommy were sitting on deck with our feet dangling in the cockpit awaiting the porridge. The cockpit was a large and handy place where we kept the compass and where we children could sit right down inside. But that day we were sitting up perkily with fearsome appetites.

Mommy put milk and a spoonful of honey into each bowl and then passed the bowls, one by one, up to me and Robin through the hatchway. Joel was ravenous and he greedily gobbled a huge spoonful of his porridge even before we had said grace. Immediately he produced a strangulated sound and made a disgusting face. His eyes squinted, his mouth crinkled, his whole body shivered with revulsion, then he leaned over the side of the boat and spat out the entire mouthful of porridge. "Horrible, awful! Yeuchhh!!" he spluttered. At the sound of this performance, Mommy's head came popping up from the cabin. "Nonsense, Joel, don't be ridiculous. It's good oatmeal. Eat it up and stop making faces!" Her head disappeared again.

Robin and I hesitated. We toyed with our spoons and stirred the porridge warily. Daddy, who by this time had his bowl, took a large mouthful, unimpressed by Joel's performance. His reaction was immediate. He spat out the porridge, and made similar strangled noises to those Joel had made. His face even looked like Joel's. They sat there, the two of them, with squinty eyes, mouths pinched, groaning and whimpering.

By now Mommy was cross. She had just spent a long time in the hot, rocking galley, cooking and dishing up the porridge. She was not amused by Joel and Daddy, and understandably, she took their reaction somewhat personally. She came stomping up on deck with her own bowl in her hand muttering, "Ridiculous, can't even eat a bit of porridge. I've never see anything so pathetic in my life." And so on. Then she took a large mouthful to prove what feeble and insipid fools Joel and Daddy were.

Her reaction was even more dramatic than their's had been. She shrieked in a gurgly sort of way, and then without a word, poured her porridge overboard. Then she grabbed Daddy's and Joel's bowls and poured out the rest of their porridge into the water. She was still making strange, anguished, throaty sounds, and her eyes were squinting just like Joel's and Daddy's. Robin and I, not to be left out, sampled a tiny bite before ours too was thrown to the fish. It was indeed foul. We all agreed it was the worst thing we had ever tasted, and that it reached new heights of gastronomic masochism.

The sea water may have looked pure and clean, but when it was heated, the millions of tiny invisible organisms had started to cook, and the taste thereof was foul and putrid beyond description.

Somehow the mixture of porridge and the sweetness of the honey only served to make the dish an even greater assault on the taste buds.

When Mommy had finished tossing our porridge to the fish, she stopped and looked at us. Slowly she started to laugh, and soon she was crying with laughter. The rest of us were laughing too, holding our sides and wiping our eyes, shrieking with new bouts of hilarity, setting each other off again and again. In the middle of the Gulf Stream, with not another soul in sight, we sailed under a beautiful clear sky, on a beautiful clear sea, laughing and laughing and laughing until we were too weak to make another sound.

CHAPTER FIVE

Freeport Harbor

Apart from the nigh deadly taste of the porridge, we arrived in the Bahamas unscathed. There was great excitement when we first spotted land after being out at sea for two days. We could see a thin line on the horizon which grew larger and took on more shape the closer we sailed. I felt as if we had discovered a new world.

In a way it was a new world for us. We had left America behind and had sailed to a foreign land. In 1960, the Bahamas were still under the Crown and were part of the British Empire. The currency was in pounds, shillings, and pence; cars drove on the left-hand side of the road; people spoke differently and had different customs. We pledged our allegiance, no longer to the flag of the United States, but to the Queen of England. We sailed into Freeport harbor with high but entirely vague expectations. All Robin and Joel and I wanted to do was to swim and play and have fun. Mommy and Daddy, on the other hand, were responsible for making sure that we ate. Daddy had been asked to manage a furniture store. Mommy found a teaching job. First, however, we had to find a place to stay.

We docked alongside one of the bustling, towering docks, and Daddy dealt with customs. He spoke to some of the officials, who gave us permission to tie up in one of the several smaller harbors. Once officially cleared, we cast off from the tall dock that had been made for gigantic bunkering freighters, not for tiny pleasure yachts. With a line of curious onlookers staring down at us, we motored away to find our special harbor. It turned out to be a long and narrow dredged-out finger of water with bare limestone cliffs and only a tired-looking dredging platform for company. We scoured the sides of the harbor trying to find a suitable place to which we could secure the boat. Finally, we settled on a section of cliff that was lower and flatter and from which it would be relatively easy for us to climb ashore. Daddy carved some steps in the cliff, so that it would be easier for us to get up and down from the road to our boat. In time Daddy also connected us up to a gas generator so that we could use our electric lights. Later we were able to share a much better and stronger electric power supply from a huge luxury yacht that came to be moored behind us.

I can remember an initial feeling of disappointment. The cliffs were so ugly and bare and there were no trees or flowering bushes welcoming us from the shore. But once we jumped ashore and scrambled up the cliff where we could see the land around the harbor, my hopes rose again. There were interesting looking piles of rocks which would be excellent for running up and down. On the far side of the piece of land was the ocean splashing up against a rough coral shoreline. That also had promise. And in the distance, further inland, were fields full of sugar cane.

There were a few houses dotted around the rims of the fields, but apart from those, we were on our own. Later we discovered an old ruined house much nearer to our boat. It had crumbling walls and no roof, with weeds choking the old doorways. Mommy and Daddy said we could use it as our own club house since it did not seem to belong to anyone and was not used for any purpose that we could see. For days we took our brooms to the house and swept out years of sand and dust and pulled up weeds and generally scampered around, fussing over the ruin. To us it was a palace.

The town of Freeport was a few miles down the road--and what a road it was. Deep cavernous potholes pitted the tarmac. An accidental dip into one of these potholes could rip out the underside of a car. Happily, Daddy started his new job as manager of the furniture shop and was allowed to drive the company truck, which was about the best vehicle for those roads.

Freeport was changing and developing all the time. Investors flocking in from America and England and Europe built huge resort hotels in the belief that Freeport would become a tourist center. It was difficult even to imagine that. Freeport was then an untidy, sprawling mass of building sites and small houses, with little to lure a tourist. But these investors were people with glittering dreams, powerful imaginations, and lots of money, and they set out to turn Freeport into a grand and enticing resort. While we were there, the gambling license was granted to the islands. It seemed as if it was also the license to go mad. More and more development was begun, and barren stretches of unused beaches were planted with palm trees and bougainvillea bushes.

The scent of gambling attracted all sorts of unsavory characters. From time to time I overheard my parents talking about what was happening to Freeport. They were worried about the way things were going, and they spoke of finding somewhere else to live. But we were to stay two years in Freeport, tied up to the limestone cliffs in the harbor. They were two years of strangeness and unfamiliarity, and for my parents, difficulties and hard work.

But for me, a seven-year-old child, each day was a new adventure, full of wonder and great excitement. It is only now, when I look back, that I remember our time in Freeport as a time when the world around us and even my own family seemed somehow out of balance, out of kilter, lacking a certain peace.

When the summer was over, we children were put into a modern one-story school in Freeport. Mommy got a job teaching there as well. We met two brothers called Bobby and David Rose. Bobby was Robin's age, and they became special friends almost immediately. David was my age, and he became best friends with me and Joel. I considered him to be my boyfriend even though we were really more like brother and sister. We swam together and sprayed each other with the hose and were perfectly comfortable in each other's company. David had blonde hair and looked like a cross between Dennis the Menace and the impish character from Mad Magazine, but I loved him dearly. We all took ballet lessons from one of the older Rose sisters. I can remember being one of the Three Fine Fishermen in my first ballet recital, complete with red yarn beard and baggy trousers.

David actually had several older brothers and sisters, some of whom were already married with children of their own. That made David and Bobby uncles, which to me seemed very exotic and special indeed. David was in my class and Bobby was in Robin's. Sometimes my older sister seemed to be almost a breed apart, even though she was only two and three-quarters years older than I, and all her friends seemed even older.

I was somewhat in awe of them, and even though she considered me to be a big pest, little did she know that often I would steer clear of her and her companions because I felt there was just too much of an age gap between us for us to be able to communicate properly. And "properly" was defined in my own special terms. To be really good friends you had to share everything and be completely open with each other. I felt this was the only way to get on with the business of true friendship. Sharing everything meant sharing experiences as well as thoughts.

One day David had come home after school to play with me and Joel. I usually shared David with Joel because David was a bit younger than I, which as far as I was concerned gave Joel partial rights to him as well. As usual we had gone out to the old deserted ruin which had become our playhouse.

To me that derelict house was a palace. I had planned its restoration, and in my mind I could see exactly how it would look once I had fixed it. I would get a new roof put on, and window panes for the holes in the walls, and fit a door again. It was going to be the coziest little cottage in the world, with red and white gingham curtains at the window, a comfortable rug on the floor, a table with four chairs around it, a single bed, and perhaps a small dresser. I reckoned that was all that anyone could need or could wish for. And, of course, I would share this house with Robin and Joel--and David. David and I would be married to each other. As far as I was concerned, we were practically married already. After all, we played together, we liked each other "best," and we were completely open and comfortable with each other. Or so I thought.

I had my first deep upset with David the afternoon we were playing in the old house. We had been there together for quite a while and it was getting close to supper time. Soon, we could hear Mommy calling us. "Coming!" we shouted back across the field and over the limestone cliff to the boat. "Coming!" I began to scamper toward the boat, but David said, "Wait a moment." He had to answer the call of nature, and he no doubt preferred to do it in open grassland rather than do battle with the stiff handle of our pump toilet.

I waited patiently for him, idly watching him, thinking no more of it than I would have had it been Joel, when suddenly I realized I had the same need. Quickly I lowered my shorts and squatted in the dusty earth, naturally expecting David to wait for me as I had waited for him. But no sooner had he seen what I was doing than he stared at me, made a strange face, and said, "Ugh."

I was devastated and confused. Could this be my almost-husband David? Could this be my friendly, open, share-everything David, with a look of scorn--or was it embarrassment--on his face? After all, I had no objections to watching him doing anything, clothed or unclothed. We had often had baths together. What did this "ugh" mean?

Quickly I finished and pulled up my shorts. I decided to confront him. "I watched you," I said, with hurt in my voice. "Yeah," he came back, "but that's different. You're a girl." Blow him, I knew I was a girl. He was a boy and I was a girl. How else were we going to get married and set up house together in the renovated ruin? But what I could not figure out was why it was all right for me to watch him going pee, but not all right for him to watch me going pee. Something wasn't quite right.

After that there was a little pocket of self-consciousness in me around David, and I did not like not being able to share everything openly with him the way we always had. Worst of all, I began to worry that there might be other areas that David would not want to share with me, and I never wanted to see that look on his face again. So some of my dreams with David died, and I stayed away from games and adventures we might have had. And I felt funny unclothed around him after that, even though, of course, we were still boyfriend and girlfriend.

Meanwhile Robin and Bobby were conducting a sensible and correct friendship. I have no idea what they did when they were all alone, but they always seemed like two good friends. In my more ruthless moments, I had to admit that while David was perfectly wonderful looking, with permanently tousled sun-bleached hair, and a broad grin across a freckled face, it was Bobby who was strictly the better looking of the two. With his dark hair and large, mischievous dark brown eyes, he was definitely a cut above just "cute."

I appreciated Bobby's handsomeness as if through a screen or a thick mist. After all, he was the same age as Robin, which made him practically ancient, and because he was Robin's special friend, he inhabited a different realm. In a way he was not entirely real to me. He was a being called "Bobby" who was not of my world, and I was perfectly content that this was so. However, one afternoon he came into my world quite unexpectedly.

Sometimes during playtime at school several of the classes would join together for a game of Red Rover. When this happened, there would be two opposing teams which would stand in straight lines facing each other, about twenty or thirty feet apart. The members of each team would grip each other tightly, hand to elbow, on down the line to form an impenetrable wall. One team captain would call out "Red Rover, Red Rover, send so and so over," naming one of the people on the opposing team. Then that person had to come away from his team, run over to the other team, and try to break through their line. If the person broke through, he got to choose someone from that team and return to his own team. If, however, he could not break through the line of bodies, he had to stay and join that team. Eventually one team would end up with most of the players, and there would only be a handful left on the other team.

On this particular afternoon Bobby was chosen to be captain of one team. The opposing captain was a nasty and foul-smelling boy called Simon, who had green moss growing on his teeth. He gave me the shivers just to look at him, much less to get close to him or to have to speak to him. Therefore, I was exceedingly pleased to be chosen by Bobby to be on his team and to note that I was among the first few picked. I knew he had chosen me because I was good at sports, I could run fast, and I was strong. Of course, he had already chosen Robin because, besides being fast and strong, she was his girlfriend.

When the teams were all picked, the calling began. At some point I was called over, and joy of joys, I managed to break through the opposing team's line. So I chose the strongest of their team and returned to my team a hero, or heroine. Play continued until we had to start afternoon classes, and by that time Bobby's team was declared the winner. I felt proud that I had contributed to our success.

Tired and happy, I walked back across the field and headed toward my classroom where my teacher, the dreaded Mrs. Glaser, would be waiting for me. I was alone and was just passing between two buildings in a somewhat secluded corner when Bobby materialized beside me. His eyes were dancing and his whole body seemed full of motion. I looked up at him and smiled, expecting him to walk by, but he didn't. Instead, he placed his hands on my shoulders, bent down, and kissed me. Then he gave me a lopsided grin and vanished.

I stood there, stunned and outraged. How dare Bobby kiss me! How dare he! He was Robin's boyfriend. What was he doing kissing me? It didn't make sense. Why would he want to kiss me anyway? I was just a little girl, someone his kid brother knew. Puzzled and disturbed by this odd occurrence, I walked on to class, cross and disappointed with Bobby and offended on behalf of Robin. I sure wouldn't want my boyfriend going off and kissing my little sister. I simply could not figure out why Bobby had kissed me. It seemed like a mistake to me.

It was not until some time later that I finally allowed logic to take its course, in spite of my protesting sensibilities. No, it did not make sense for Bobby to kiss me, unless--and this is what really upset me--Bobby had wanted to kiss me. I had dismissed the possibility that it had been a case of mistaken identity. Bobby had looked me straight in the eyes before doing the terrible deed. And I had also dismissed the possibility that it had been a dare, something one of his friends had challenged him to do. Somehow the way he had caught me when we were all alone, and the excitement in his eyes, and the strange smile on his face had convinced even me that no one was forcing him to do this. Therefore, it had to be an act done of his own free will for whatever reason. "He probably just got carried away because I helped the team," I muttered to myself, but I didn't really believe that even then.

I struggled hard to come to terms with Bobby's kiss. It seemed to open up a whole new and murky world where things that were plain and straightforward were no longer so. The strangest thing was how guilty I felt when I thought about Robin. But I knew

I did not need to feel guilty; after all, it was not I who had sought out Bobby. It rankled and nagged at me, and I wrestled with it until my quiet outrage gave way to a grudging acceptance of the facts, which in time gave birth to a strange new sensation: a shy and halting feeling of secret pride. No, I did not approve of what Bobby had done, and of course I would never ever mention it to him or to anyone else, but it was rather special to have been kissed by an older boy, and my sister's boyfriend at that. Life had begun to be slightly confusing and somewhat unpredictable but certainly more intriguing and even more of a grand adventure.

CHAPTER SIX

Fantasies and Phobias

I don't know about any other seven-year-olds, but by the time we had moored at Freeport, I was beginning to have some rather interesting thoughts. I cannot remember how it started, but for some reason I developed a great affection for goats. Most days I spent all the hours I could running and playing on the piles of dredged coral rock that had been dumped on the wasteland near where we were moored.

It was not entirely barren; there were the few small fields of sugar cane and, on the ocean side of the harbor, the spiky coral reefs. These reefs stuck out of the water and were filled with crabs and sea plants and other squirmy things. They were as sharp as knives, and we were not supposed to play on them barefoot or alone.

I loved the vast mounds of the coral rock rubble. I can remember hopping from clump to clump and scrabbling to the tops of these hills to survey the land and sea around me. From the tops I could see the huge freighters coming and going from the harbor. I could see them as they became dots on the horizon. I felt like a brave explorer with worlds to conquer.

During this time I must have met a neighbor who had a goat, or perhaps I'd read a book about goats. I thought about goats with sweet faces, goats that could leap and bound from rock to rock and never miss a step; goats that could eat branches of trees, old cardboard boxes, and paper. I even wrote a poem about a goat.

One day when Robin and Joel must have been playing elsewhere together, I sneaked a box of tissues from my mother's shelf and raced to the hills. I bounded to the top of one and squatted down, clutching the tissue box. My heart was pounding. I was thrilled and excited. I was a goat!

I took the first tissue and started nibbling a corner. It tasted rather nice, even though it was a bit difficult to swallow. I ate it all. I took out the second tissue and started chewing. After a while my goat jaws began to struggle. The tissue melted into soggy wads of pulp which were beginning to stick in my throat. I looked into the box. There were an awful lot of tissues left, and then there was the box! I knew that a goat would eat the box as well. I wondered how long it would take me to eat my first goat meal. The lumps of paper in my mouth were becoming harder to swallow, and they tasted sort of funny. I chewed on, staring out to sea, thinking goat thoughts.

Just then I heard the sound of my mother's voice. She was calling my name, "Christina! Christina!" and then, "Lunch!" Quickly I spat out my mouthful of tissue, grabbed the box, and leaped down the hill. By the time I had climbed aboard and slid hurriedly into place around the table, on which the most delicious-looking lunch I had ever seen was laid out, I had come to the somewhat disappointed and reluctant but firm and unshakable conclusion that I really was not a goat!

Freeport harbor was always busy. The huge tankers would lie outside the harbor and wait for the tenders to come out to them. Some vessels would make their way through the treacherous coral reefs into the harbor to unload their cargo. One of these cargo ships came all the way into our section of the harbor, and tied up against the hacked limestone cliffs across from us.

One day, after I had stopped thinking I was a goat, Robin, Joel, David Rose, and I walked around to see the massive ship. One of the sailors saw us staring up at the ship with wide eyes and invited us onto the floating mountain.

The four of us made our way up the swaying gangplank, thrilled to our bones. During our tour of the deck, we saw a group of young British sailors leaping off the railings into the water. We watched the men jump off and land with a splash some thirty feet below. They looked so small down in the water from way up on the deck. Immediately Robin and Joel and David wanted to try the jump overboard. Sensibly, one of the sailors suggested that we ask our mother first. Besides, we were not in our swimming gear.

We raced off the ship and flew around the harbor's edge to our boat. We asked Mommy if we could go back to the ship, and miraculously she agreed. We tore into our swimming things and ran back to the ship.

I say "we" because, although I did as the others did, inside I was not happy, not happy at all. In all the excitement everyone, including my uncannily perceptive mother, had failed to notice my lack of true enthusiasm. Inside I was frightened, churning with fear. Those men had looked so tiny when they hit the water; tiny men making large splashes miles below. I didn't know if I would like the feel of hitting the water after a thirty-foot jump. What if the water felt like concrete?

What if I landed in a funny position? What if . . .? My mind was racing with dreadful possibilities.

Back on the ship, Robin and Joel and David clambered up on to the railing and stood there teetering and laughing and teasing each other about who would be the first to go. Then they all jumped together, giggling and shrieking with delight. I looked down. I decided I would jump. After all, everyone who had jumped was fine and had come up and done it again. But a moment later I changed my mind. No, it was too far to jump. But then again, maybe . . . I carried on in this state of indecision, feeling embarrassed and ashamed. Everyone around me was encouraging me to jump, explaining how easy it was. I knew it was easy, I just was not sure it was nice. I stood there trying to gather my courage until, suddenly, it was too late. The sailors were called, and they had to stop their jumping, dry off, and get back to work. The sailor who had first invited us on board led us back down the gangplank and gave us many friendly waves good-bye.

Robin and Joel and David were laughing and dripping and chattering about the fun they had had. I walked beside them, quiet with disappointment. By the time we got back to the boat, the others were exhausted, exhilarated, and ravenous. I sat subdued, and, mercifully, ignored while they compared their jumping stories.

Later my mother asked me why I had not jumped. I answered simply, "I didn't want to," which was not entirely false. Of course, I wished I had jumped so that I could say that I had. But really I had not wanted to jump off the side of that ship. It had just seemed too risky to me.

Not taking the plunge off the ship proved to be an early indication of my dislike of heights, particularly when the height is at the edge of a steep drop or a precipice. In due course I would be able to add a fear of lightning and of sharks to my budding fear of heights. All these fears were not developed out of the blue. They took years of many scary times when lightning storms crackled and crashed right over me or when I had a few close calls with sharks. These experiences, combined with my always overactive imagination, created lasting and very real fears.

CHAPTER SEVEN

Fattie Pie and Sweetie Pie

We were not always the only boat tied up to the limestone cliffs in our part of the harbor. From time to time we shared the space with a rather grand motor boat. This boat, or yacht, to be proper, was huge. It towered above us, and its prow seemed to look down at our boat through its porthole eyes as if to say, "Now you're with the big boys." The upper decks of the boat were enclosed by endless glass windows which were continually being polished by one of the numerous crew. From time to time a bird would try to fly across the upper deck, unaware of the glass. Usually the birds died instantly, but every so often they would be merely stunned.

On two separate occasions, specimens of a cheery little bird called the banaquit tried to fly through the glass and failed, but without fatal consequences. The captain, who was very friendly toward us, brought us the tiny crumpled and stunned birds. Both were babies and were brought to us within days of each other. They must have been just learning to fly. One was sleek with a lovely tail but almost no wings. The other was a plump little soul with well formed wings but almost no tail feathers. The one with the tail we called Sweetie Pie, and the other we called Fattie Pie. After an initial recovery period they became healthy and perky.

Daddy constructed a large cage out of a spare bit of screening and a wooden box frame. They spent nights in their cage, but they spent much of the days hopping and perching and chirping around the main cabin. Because the birds were so young, they were perfectly happy living with humans and quickly learned how to get what they wanted. Usually they wanted a banana or some other fruit, but sometimes they wanted a game of hide-and-go-seek around our shoulders and under our hair. Then they would hop beneath our hair on our collars and peek out and chirp, with only their tiny beaks and bright eyes visible in our tangled manes.

We learned how to feed them bananas from our mouths. Joel was being silly and had about half a banana sticking out of his mouth, when suddenly one of the birds hopped onto the banana and started pecking at it. After that, we always fed them bananas that way.

Freeport was used as a refueling station for the gargantuan supertankers, which would come as close as they could to the shore to be met by the link-up ships. Inevitably there were spills, and when this happened, the oil would cover the surface of the water and even float into our finger of the harbor. Then the waterline of our boat would be engulfed with thick, sticky, smelly tar. It was awful. The sides of our boat became covered with a black film as the water lapped at our hull. Sometimes the ropes holding us to the shore would slacken at high tide and dip into the slimy mess. That made my father very angry; it took hours of rubbing them down with a special solution to get them clean again.

Sometimes the oil was so thick that it carried objects on top of it, like bottles and old shoes and pieces of clothing, and worst of all, dead birds and fish. Gulls were the most common birds killed this way. Gulls love to sit on the sea way out from land and catch fish, and they were particularly vulnerable to the cloying tar. Their tarred and blackened bodies, lying mangled on top of a floating, reeking island of tar, would bump into our boat. We all hated the tar.

Unfortunately, Sweetie Pie and Fattie Pie were learning to fly. Sometimes they made the cliff, and then Joel would go scampering ashore and fetch them back. Other times, though, they would lose altitude and end up in the water. This was not serious if the harbor was clean, but it was disastrous on the occasions when they fell into the tar. We would fish them out instantly with our fishing net on a pole, but they would be covered in the slime and gasping for breath. Mommy would wash them lovingly and rinse them in clean fresh water. Miraculously, they survived all their dunkings into the tar.

We knew we could not keep the birds forever. Sweetie Pie was actually beginning to grow some proper wings, and Fattie Pie looked less and less like a ball of down. Mommy and Daddy had explained to us that there would come a time when we would have to say goodbye to our friends. We understood with our heads if not with our hearts.

Sweetie Pie was the first to go. One day as we were sitting on the deck talking and playing, he spread his wings and sailed off to the shore. At first we thought this time was like all the others. But this time he did not wait on the shore and call for us. He paused for a moment, then took off again and disappeared over the fields of sugar cane and the sandy road leading away from the water's edge.

Sweetie Pie was gone. We looked for him for several days, half expecting to find him perching on the deck one morning, demanding a banana. But he never came back.

Fattie Pie seemed less inclined to leave us, even though he was getting larger and flying confidently around our rigging. One morning Mommy and Daddy told us they had found a home for Fattie Pie, a large nursery with hundreds of trees and flowers that was almost like a nature preserve. Fattie Pie, who had grown so accustomed to people, would be safe there. The owners could keep an eye out for him and chat to him if he still wanted human company. We knew this was for the best.

Our family set off in the car with Fattie Pie hopping from shoulder to shoulder, tickling our necks and trying to peck our ears. When we got to the nursery, a man came out to meet us. He was delighted to see Fattie Pie and assured us that the sweet, trusting bird would have a paradise in which to live. Fattie Pie flew out of the car and up into the jungle of green where we left him chirping happily. Robin and Joel and I cried all the way home, and I think Mommy and Daddy did as well.

CHAPTER EIGHT

Mistress Glaser

Mrs. Glaser was my teacher during our stay at Freeport. I would have been seven when I started at Freeport School. Mrs. Glaser was not like the lovely Miss Rose Cormier of Boca Raton, the only other teacher I had ever had. Rather, Mrs. Glaser was of the old school, a prim and proper lady, thin and gray, with a rod of iron for a backbone. As far as I can remember, nothing ever amused her.

Mrs. Glaser ruled over our class with a chilly and distant efficiency, but even her attitude could not dampen my enthusiasm for school. I loved sitting at my desk and working. I loved writing on clean sheets of paper. Our classroom had maps on the walls, a globe, and blackboards at the front of the room. There were about twenty of us, and we each had our own flip-top desk.

The school had been built about two years earlier, and a new wing had just been added. It was a single-story building, modern and utilitarian, now in the shape of a large "L." There were four classes and forty-five pupils in all. The school had been built on a vast empty lot. There were houses rimming this large piece of land, but there was still a good deal of empty field at the back of the school.

Despite Mrs. Glaser, I loved school. I loved adding up the pounds, shillings, and pence for our sums. I loved music and singing, playing the recorder, writing, spelling, geography, and reading. I especially loved reading. I read everything and anything I could find. One day, however, my reading got me into trouble.

During the session before lunch, Mrs. Glaser asked our class to choose a book from the school library, read it, and be prepared to talk about it. Many of the books were slim Penguin volumes. I went to the bookshelf and chose several Penguins.

I read the first book. I opened a second and read that too. I read a third and a fourth. Because I had read through my stack of books and there was still some time before lunch, I went up to ask Mrs. Glaser if I could choose another book.

"Mrs. Glaser," I asked, "may I please get another book?" Mrs. Glaser gave me a sour look. "Have you finished yours already?" "Yes, Mrs. Glaser, I've finished all of them." "All of them?" she asked archly. "How many have you read?" "I've read four, Mrs. Glaser," I answered.

"Four!" Mrs. Glaser glared at me, and then spat out loudly,

"You're lying! How dare you lie to me?" I froze and winced. By this time, of course, most of the class had stopped reading, and having heard Mrs. Glaser's voice, they sensed a scene. I had never stood up to a teacher before. I had never had to. I hated confrontations, and I couldn't understand why Mrs. Glaser was being so unreasonable. "I have read four books," I said in a weak voice. She stared at me for a moment, then she pushed back her chair and stood up. She cleared her throat loudly and addressed the class, who by now had given up all pretense of reading.

"Christina tells me that she has read four books just now," she began in a mocking voice, and then added fiercely, "THAT IS A LIE! It would have been impossible for her to have read four books, now, wouldn't it? SHE IS LYING TO ME! I hope no one else is thinking of lying to me." There was a dramatic pause. "Christina must be punished for lying. It is a wicked thing to do."

To my horror she opened the drawer in her desk and drew out a wooden ruler. She grabbed one of my hands and held it high for everyone else to see. Then she turned it over and hit me with the ruler across the back of my wrist. She hit very hard and kept on hitting again and again. I had never been punished in school before, and it hurt doubly that I was being punished for a crime I had not committed.

I was so shocked that I did not cry, even though my wrist stung horribly and my embarrassment was acute. Rather, I felt quite calm and clear inside, and I found myself viewing the situation as if from a distance. I saw a bitter old woman lashing out at a young girl, and I found the spectacle pathetic. Suddenly I felt sorry for Mrs. Glaser, for her frustration, her resentment, and her lack of understanding. It did not matter any more what she did to me. I realized that she could never hurt me.

At last Mrs. Glaser dropped my hand. Her whole body was shaking. She sat down quickly and without looking at me said, "You will read all the books you have said that you have read, you will write a report on each of them, and you will stay in during lunch if you have not finished."

I went back to my desk with my wrist bright red and burning with pain. It did hurt, but it didn't bother me. I sat down and picked up the first book I had read and started to read it again. I had written most of the report on the first book by the time lunch was called. There was instant noise and happy confusion as all the other children snapped their books shut and bustled out of the classroom. I kept writing for a little while, before I sneaked a glance up at Mrs. Glaser. She was stacking papers and seemed to have recovered her composure. The impenetrable, efficient, slightly disapproving look was once again firmly in place.

I went back to my writing. I began to feel self-conscious, sitting at my desk with only Mrs. Glaser in the room, and I began to think of my lunch. I thought of playtime and my friends. My wrist was still stinging, and a tiny prick of anger began to grow in me. I wrote more quickly.

Just then Mrs. Glaser spoke in a dry and flat voice. "You may go now," she said. That was all. She did not ask to see my report, or demand that I finish the reports later, or threaten me with further punishment, just "You may go now" with her head down, preoccupied. I tidied my desk and flew out of the classroom, free. After that Mrs. Glaser behaved as if the incident had never taken place. But I could never trust her again and never again went to her with little stories or things of interest to me.

My mother said that Mrs. Glaser behaved like that because she disliked Americans and because she was threatened by my cleverness. This explanation only confused me further. I could not understand how someone could dislike a person just because of where they came from, and I could not work out at all why a teacher would be threatened by one of her pupils' cleverness. All I had sensed was that Mrs. Glaser had wanted to hit me until I broke, or until I went away. I got the feeling that she wished I did not exist. And I also got the feeling that something was all bottled up inside her, because she hit me with almost uncontrolled rage-- much too ferocious a reaction to my supposed crime. Luckily the experience did not mar my feelings about school, teachers, or learning, but it did start my first feelings of caution toward adults.

CHAPTER NINE

The Death and Burial
of Tammy

We acquired a Siamese kitten soon after coming to Freeport. Ever since Tipsy had jumped ship in Atlantic Highlands, we children had begged Mommy and Daddy for another cat. Now, in Freeport, it seemed safe to get a new pet. We named the kitten Tammy, after the song, which none of us could sing through completely--but we all knew the last line, which went "Tammy's in love." So little Tammy came aboard.

She took to the boat instantly as if she had been born at sea. There were so many places to hide and many comfortable corners in which to curl up and take a nap. She was fond of the sail bags which were stored at the front of the boat in the bow storage section. She was fond of our shelves where she would disappear for hours, and she patronized our bunks as well. Tammy soon learned to jump from our boat to the shore, and we became used to the sound of a dainty thud on the deck signaling that Tammy had come home. She fell overboard a few times too, but did not seem to be put off life afloat. On shore she caught birds and mice and generally had a grand time.

I believe that it takes superhuman effort to get along with one's family anywhere, but especially on a small boat. Since none of us were superhuman, occasionally the atmosphere aboard was tense, and it varied from icy cold to red hot. At times it exploded, particularly between my parents. Most of the time they were wonderful. They only had each other, they were responsible for us children, and we lived a fairly precarious life. There was really not anyone to whom they could turn. The only support system they had was the occasional friend we would make on our travels, and the loving thoughts and prayers and letters from friends and family back in America. But sometimes the pressures, frustrations, and feelings of loneliness became too much, especially for my mother, and she would go to pieces. Mommy, who was outwardly serene and placid, had a fiery temper when provoked. In certain moods she was like a wounded tigress. Sometimes, when the anger or hurt and frustration coincided, the result was fairly spectacular.

Daddy, on the other hand, was just the opposite. Although he was rarely wildly exuberant, he was typically content, wrapped up in his own thoughts. Much of the time he whistled to himself, a happy tuneful whistle. When times were bad for him, he went inward with the problem and became remote and lost in private thought. When he was like this, he would literally not even hear when someone would call to him, or ask him a question. Unfortunately, I developed a similar capacity when reading. Deep in a book, I would suddenly be jolted by my mother shouting "Christina! This is the last time I'm calling you!" I realize now what an irritating trait it can be. And so, when my mother met my father head on, there could be fireworks and hazardous fallout.

My parents attempted to keep their disagreements hidden from us, but it was impossible for sound not to carry, especially when everyone was within a few feet of each other. On the nights when my parents argued, Robin and Joel and I would lie in our bunks, tense and worried, hating the sound of their voices rising louder and louder, becoming more and more venomous. There would be pauses, sarcasm, another verbal attack, and so on.

I used to lie frozen still, straining to hear the words so that I could understand exactly what it was they were arguing about. And I used to pray like mad, "Please God, make them stop. Make them love each other." I felt there must be something that I could do to help, to take away these horrible times when the whole world felt broken and shattered. But the arguments went on, sometimes over several nights.

One day after school, we met Daddy at the furniture warehouse and we all drove home together. During the drive an argument erupted between my parents. They did not seem to be aware that we were in the back seat listening to every word. Maybe they were past caring. The strained expressions, the terse replies, and the anger confused us children. It felt like a thunderstorm brewing. By the time we got back to the boat, Mommy and Daddy had abandoned all restraint, and the harsh words were flying fast and hard between them.

Robin and Joel hated these times as much as I did. Joel would wring his hands and burst into tears, unable to cope with the vehemence of it all. Robin would go silent, and her face would become dark and sad. I usually tried to moderate, to play umpire, and when I grew older sometimes they would listen to me, and even later, I was used as a mediator or a go-between.

But that night our tearful pleading of "Stop and say you're sorry!" had no effect. We children scattered to our bunks, sobbing and moaning, while my parents lashed at each other with their words, and cut each other to shreds with cruel accusations.

It had gone too far. All of a sudden my father threw back the hatch cover, bolted up the ladder and jumped off the boat. Seconds later there was the sound of an engine roaring to life, and finally the sound of the truck disappearing at speed down the pothole-ridden road. Mommy was limp with hurt and anger, and now she was also frightened. Their arguments had never ended with one of them storming off. It had been like an unwritten rule, "Thou shalt not run away." But Daddy and truck were gone. We all sobbed and hugged Mommy, and worried that Daddy would never come back. We loved them both and we were desperate for them to love each other. Finally, Mommy tucked us back in our bunks and went to bed herself.

The morning dawned too soon and too bright. Mommy's face had the drained look of someone who had been crying for most of the night. It felt strange and awful not to have Daddy with us, and depression hung over us like a thick bank of fog. It must have been Saturday, because we stayed home that day, free for a day of play that none of us could enjoy. At some point that morning we noticed that Tammy was not around. She had not demanded her breakfast in her usual loud, insistent voice. We went ashore, calling her name, promising her an extra helping. She did not come, and we thought little more about it. Occasionally, Tammy would wander off and arrive back a day or so later, starving hungry and wildly affectionate.

Later that afternoon Daddy came back. The atmosphere was worse, not better. Even though we were all relieved to see him, there was still a chill between him and mother, which they seemed too tired or still too angry to try to dispel. Daddy spoke little and busied himself with jobs around the boat. There was no whistling that day.

By the evening, the atmosphere had eased a bit and we started to relax again. Tammy had still not returned, and we now were getting a bit worried. Mommy went ashore and spent some time calling her, but no cat. Tammy did not come home the following day either. We were now very concerned about her. Daddy went to the neighbors, the farmers with the fields of sugar cane, to ask if they had seen Tammy, but they had not. There was nothing to do but wait.

When we went to school on Monday, some people who lived close by spoke to Mommy and we discovered where Tammy had been. On Friday night, the night of the argument, Tammy must have been sneaking a nap in the back of the furniture truck which we kept parked close to the boat. When Daddy had roared off in the truck, unwittingly he must have taken Tammy. Daddy had spent the night in the truck parked not far from our school. At some point Tammy must have jumped out of the back of the truck.

Two days later the family who lived near the school had found Tammy's body in their garden. She had been attacked and killed by their German shepherd dog. When we heard this news we were inconsolable. It was a particularly desolate grief, because we knew that Tammy would still be alive if it had not been for Mommy and Daddy's argument. I felt worse about showing my sadness because I knew it pointed an accusing finger at my parents and their behavior on Friday night. It was awful: we would never forget Tammy, and now, we could never forget the argument.

The people who found Tammy gave us her body, which was torn and already stiff. Robin and Joel and I asked if we could bury Tammy in the empty field of weeds at the back of the school. Mommy and Daddy said we could. The three of us, tears running down our cheeks, prepared the grave. We dug a hole in the sandy earth large enough to hold Tammy and lined it with wild flowers. Gently we laid Tammy down on her floral bower, and pushed the sand back over her. On the top of her grave we planted more wild flowers picked from the field, and the small mound glowed with color. Somehow, it made us feel better about Tammy. Over the next few days my parents made up and the sadness lifted from our family. We were free again, free to enjoy ourselves and get on with life.

About a week after we buried Tammy we were struck with the desire to check up on her, to see if all was well with the grave. Robin and Joel and I took a few of our friends one day after school to visit the grave. The mound had sunk a bit and all the bright flowers were brown and shrivelled. It made us sad again. One of our friends was something of a ruffian. "I bet your cat isn't even in there," he taunted, "I bet you just put flowers there to pretend." "That's not true" we exploded. "Tammy's in there. We buried her." "I don't believe you," the creepy child said. "Prove it."

Our honor was at stake. Without hesitation we started digging. Suddenly we spotted a hard, long, pointed object protruding out of the soil. It was Tammy's tail, rigid and covered in dirt. We dug around the tail and uncovered the rest of the poor cat. She was stiff and filthy and she stank. She stank stupefyingly. Our friend was most impressed. His eyes bugged out and he stepped back, frightened and repulsed, but very impressed. Our honor was saved, and immediately we became mini-heroes, figures of intrigue and bravery and all manner of disgusting things. Not only had we buried a cat, but we had fearlessly dug her up again.

We covered Tammy over for the second time and replaced the dead flowers with fresh ones, carefully picking the blossoms and planting the broken stems in the soil on top of the mound.

When our parents found out about our activities, as they inevitably did, we received only a mild scolding. Tammy's death was still a sensitive subject for them. When I think back, my parents must have been going through a rather bad patch, because I remember many arguments. Tammy's death definitely did not help. Of course, at the time, it was just life, and one did not think of one's parents going through patches, good or bad.

CHAPTER TEN

Cabin Boy

A few weeks before our first Easter in Freeport, a package came for us. It was sent from our grandparents in California. Grandmother had made beautiful new dresses for me and Robin and Mommy. Later in Freeport, Mommy bought a straw bonnet each for Robin and me to go with our dresses. My dress was pink with tiny white flowers on it and a large lacy collar. Robin's dress was exactly the same, only blue. Our straw hats had small brims and round crowns with colored ribbons and flowers. When I got up on Easter morning and put on my new clothes, I felt too excited and pretty for words. The dresses were slightly gauzy and made soft rustles when we moved. We had new shoes too, white sandals. That new outfit made me so happy I nearly burst.

We went to a church in Freeport of which I remember nothing, and then my parents announced that they had a surprise for us. Grinning and giggling, they drove us down dusty roads, pitted with the ubiquitous potholes, until we came out at another end of the harbor. This was the business end of Freeport Harbor, with trucks and derrick cranes and piles of freight next to the huge ships tied to the docks. Men were everywhere, shouting and calling to each other.

We got out of the truck and walked over to one of the smaller ships, a bedraggled-looking vessel. My father hailed one of the crew and went off and talked with him, while Mommy stayed with us and refused to answer our endless stream of questions. Finally Daddy came back to us with a slightly lopsided and self-conscious grin on his face. "Come on, Kiddliwinks," he said, and led us to the edge of the dock right above the tired-looking ship. There on the deck standing next to a small pile of twigs was the skinniest, most pitiful-looking donkey we had ever seen. Mommy let out a little gasp, her face containing both horror and humor.

The animal was painfully thin, but there was something undeniably comical about the way it stared up at us, munching the bare twigs. That donkey was our surprise. He had been shipped miles on the boat from an island called Rum Cay. Mommy and Daddy had heard that one could get donkeys from Rum Cay and had arranged for one to be brought to us. Evidently our donkey was supposed to have come earlier, but now at last he had arrived. We all knew immediately what his name should be: "Cabin Boy."

Cabin Boy was hoisted off the deck of the ship and lifted into the back of our truck. Daddy tied him so he would not be thrown about as we made the bumpy ride back around the harbor to our own little mooring area. We washed and fed Cabin Boy and lovingly brushed his bony sides. We let him graze in the fields near our boat, which were covered in coarse grasses and tasty daisies.

Within a week or two Cabin Boy was a different animal. His once-sunken sides now bulged, and he could kick up his heels and gallop around on the end of his rope. When Cabin Boy saw one of us coming, he would bray enormous hiccupping brays. We took him for long walks and tried to ride him, but Cabin Boy was not convinced that he was meant to be ridden. His ears would go back and he would break into an impossible gallop, interspersed with bucking and braying. The rider would inevitably end up in the dust with a sore bottom and skinned palms. But it did not matter to us. We would climb up again for another short but exciting ride, only to be thrown again.

Once Cabin Boy threw Daddy, and Daddy hobbled around for days with a sore back. Cabin Boy threw everyone. Even Mommy, a horsewoman since birth, was no match for Cabin Boy. But we all adored him, despite his refusal to be ridden for more than a few minutes at a time. Everyone who met Cabin Boy loved him, except for the farming family who lived a little way down the road.

The farming family grew fields of sugar cane and some vegetables. Cabin Boy learned fairly quickly how to chew through his rope and escape. This he did often, and he would gallop to the neighbors' sugar cane fields for a day of blissful munching. This made the farmer furious. He would come running up beside our boat and shout at us, "Youse donkey in my fields, eating all my sugar cane!" Then we children would be sent, new rope in hand, to fetch him back. Cabin Boy was a credit to his breed, and sometimes we would have to drag him the whole way, while he kept his legs straight and skidded behind us like an ice skater on bumpy ice. As much as Cabin Boy hated being nabbed and brought home in disgrace, it did not stop him from running away. Daddy kept on inventing new and better ways of tying him to his stake, but Cabin Boy always found a way to break loose. After a while the neighbor would just capture Cabin Boy and tie him up in his own garden with a few stalks of sugar cane to pacify him until we could come and get him.

Cabin Boy was our beloved friend while we lived in Freeport, but we could not take him with us when it was time to leave. My parents had grown tired of Freeport, tired of the bumpy roads and the ugly developments springing up all around us, weary of being tied up to the barren limestone cliffs. Even though Daddy's furniture store was quite successful, the American owners had recently sold it, and the new owners wanted to operate it themselves. It was time to move on.

My parents had met a man named Gil Drake who had built a sports-fishing club on his own tiny island. He asked them to come and manage the club for him. After visiting the island and deciding upon the terms of employment, my parents accepted the offer. Our new home would be a small island called Deep Water Cay off the east coast of Grand Bahama, far away from the wheeling and dealing of Freeport. The *Tappan Zee* could be moored off the island's dock. We children were told of the white sandy beaches and the plentiful fish and shells. It sounded good to us, and we all wanted to go. But we did not want to leave Cabin Boy behind.

Joel could not understand why we could not tie him on deck for the trip. It was going to be a two-day sail at least, and Mommy and Daddy thought it would not be fair to have Cabin Boy on the boat for that length of time. But Joel felt that Cabin Boy would rather be seasick with us than homesick without us. In the light of what was to happen to Cabin Boy, it probably would have been better if we had taken him with us, but of course we could not know the fate that was to befall him.

We knew vaguely of a lively family with lots of children who lived near a field. Mommy and Daddy asked them if they would like to have Cabin Boy. They were delighted. The father offered to collect Cabin Boy a few days before we were to leave Freeport. On the agreed day we got up early and ran to Cabin Boy to give him all the hugs and strokes we could fit in before the father arrived. The family lived about ten miles down the road, and we assumed that they would bring a trailer to transport Cabin Boy. But when the father arrived, he had just brought his ordinary car and a length of rope. Daddy helped to tie Cabin Boy to the back of the car. "You've got to take it very slowly," Daddy said to the man. "Keep him at a slow trot or walk." "Sure, sure," the man said with a grin, "I know all about donkeys."

We flung our arms around Cabin Boy's neck for the last time and kissed him on his soft muzzle. Then we stepped back and waved him goodbye. The man slid into the driver's seat and revved the engine. "Bye, Cabin Boy," we all called, "Bye!" The man started down the road, bumping over the rocky surface. "That's good," my father shouted. "That's fast enough." The man evidently was not listening, and the car began to gather speed. Cabin Boy, who had started off at a brisk trot, was now galloping clumsily over the rough road to keep up with the car. His neck was being pulled at a funny angle and his eyes were wild. "That's fast enough!" Daddy shouted. "Slow down!" Mommy yelled. "Slow down, you jerk!" But the car kept on going faster and faster. Cabin Boy stumbled. He was struggling harder to keep up. He stumbled again, and this time he lost his footing and fell onto the road. To our horror, the car kept on driving over the bumpy road, now dragging Cabin Boy by the neck. We shrieked and jumped up and down and started to run after the car, shouting and waving our arms.

Mommy and Daddy raced after the car, impotently waving their arms in a vain attempt to attract the man's attention. Both Mommy and Daddy were swearing, something they rarely did. Finally, the car bumped to a halt. Mommy and Daddy raced over to Cabin Boy. He was lying limply on his side, breathing heavily. His legs were crumpled grotesquely under him. All of them were broken.

Cabin Boy tried to raise his head but he was too weak and in too much pain. Daddy quickly untied him from the car and told Mommy to stay with him. Then Daddy went tearing like a mad man back to the boat, more upset than I had ever seen him. Mommy stayed with Cabin Boy, weeping over him and stroking him, saying "It's all right" over and over again. The man was standing awkwardly beside Cabin Boy. "Hell," he said nervously, loudly, "why the hell can't that donkey run?"

Mommy ignored him and kept on stroking Cabin Boy. Then Daddy was back. He was holding his large pistol. The sight of the gun sent us children into shrieks of horror. Mommy and Daddy nodded to each other and Mommy stepped back from Cabin Boy, her face shiny with tears. She came over to where the three of us were huddled and put her arms around us. Daddy knelt down next to Cabin Boy's head and fired the pistol. Cabin Boy gave a twitch and then lay still, a bent, misshapen heap of soft brown fur lying in the middle of the dusty road.

To this day I do not know how Daddy resisted shooting the man. I am sure Daddy does not know either. Somehow he managed to speak to the man without killing him. We children watched as they loaded Cabin Boy's body into the back of the car. The man was by now quiet, apologetic, lost for words. "I'll see to him," he told us. "I'll bury him." My father nodded, and the man drove off, this time more slowly, with Cabin Boy's legs dangling out of the back.

The five of us walked back to the boat, hysterical with grief and anger. Words came tumbling out of our mouths, wild words.

"I'll kill him, I'll kill him," was what we children were shouting, over and over. Mommy hugged us and sobbed. Daddy had a face like granite, and his lips were pinched into a small thin line. His pale blue eyes were bright aquamarine with tears. He put the pistol away and sat quietly with us as we shouted bitter words of death to the man.

A few days later, the day before we were to leave Freeport, Daddy ran into the man by accident. He and Mommy had decided they would not see him again, even though they wanted to know where he had buried Cabin Boy, for despite our repeated urgings to kill the man, our parents realized there was nothing they could do. Cabin Boy was dead.

Daddy came home from his unexpected meeting with more horrible news: the man had not buried Cabin Boy as he had said he would. Instead, he had tipped out the body at the nearby rubbish dump. Our precious Cabin Boy had been dumped onto a heap of reeking and rotting trash, old cars and chairs, to be dealt with by the scavenging vultures by day and the fiendish rats by night. That news nearly destroyed us. We sailed out of Freeport Harbor the next day, numbed, angry, in turmoil, glad only to be getting away from the monstrous man to whom even Mommy was now muttering death.

We grieved over Cabin Boy for a long time, and only hesitantly could we speak about him, remembering the happiness, his mischief in the sugar cane fields, his bucking and braying, and his soft loving eyes. The images of his death took a long time to lose their potency. Now it is easier to tell wonderful stories of Cabin Boy's exploits in the neighbor's fields and of how none of us could stay on his back for more than a few minutes, but it is still not easy to tell of his death. The way in which this gentle creature met his end will forever stand to me as an example of man's insensitivity and stupidity, his brutality to other living creatures.

CHAPTER ELEVEN

Deep Water Cay

We sailed southeastward along the coast of Grand Bahama. The fresh sea air blew through the boat and through our souls and took away some of the sting of Cabin Boy's death. We were glad to leave Freeport, glad to leave behind the tar-clogged harbor, the frantic building, the greed of the investors, but most of all, the bitter memory of Cabin Boy's last day. As we sailed we fell into the healing rhythm and demands of the sea, and we looked forward with great excitement to Deep Water Cay.

When we sailed into the harbor at Deep Water Cay, I thought we had come to heaven. The seas were crystal clear, and I could see right to the bottom. Fish darted here and there, and shy crawfish made for cover as the *Tappan Zee* sliced silently through their world.

Deep Water Cay was a small island, only about one mile long and a quarter of a mile wide at its widest point. The one wooden dock stuck out from the island in the shape of a "T." We pulled up gently to the dock, and Daddy jumped ashore and made us fast. The *Tappan Zee* had found a new home.

We were met by a group of Bahamians who had gathered on the dock. They welcomed us with broad grins and friendly faces. They seemed to like me and Robin and Joel and pinched our cheeks and stroked our smooth hair. I could not understand their broad dialect, but I smiled back up at them, sensing their good will toward us.

One side of Deep Water Cay looked out to sea. It was a continuous stretch of soft pink-white sand, covered with beautiful shells and rimmed with a graceful fringe of golden sea oats. Sea oats only vaguely resemble ordinary oats. The heads of the tall rushes are about the length of a large hand with the individual oats clustered together in small leaf-like shapes. Sea oats grow to over six feet tall and droop gently over the hot sand and rustle in the breezes.

Besides the sea oats there were many wonderful plants and trees. My favorite was the sea grape tree. Its bark is smooth, and the branches are twisted and curved, sprouting thick leaves like large round fans. At certain times of the year the fruit would appear. Sea grapes are dark purple with firm flesh. They can be eaten raw, but we liked them best made into sea grape jam.

There were also the cocoplum bushes, short and wiry, with small glossy leaves. The white plumlike fruit is sweet and delicate, somewhat like a lychee, but not quite as moist and not so heavily perfumed.

There were also several types of palm tree, the tall yucca, and the large, graceful Australian pine. There was the dreaded poisonwood tree, which, when touched, would produce a painful red rash. And there were many types of vines and creepers and all sorts of succulents, the most striking being the barbed century plant. Even though the plants were beautiful, many of them were prickly or poisonous, and we learned not to touch or pick them indiscriminately.

We discovered that we were to be the only permanent residents on the island. The guests came and went in their private yachts or their amphibian planes. The staff motored in their small boats from Macleans Town on nearby Grand Bahama, just about a quarter of a mile away across the shallow sand flats. Gil Drake, the owner, lived in Florida. He had built a club house and several separate cabins for guests as well as a private house for himself and one for his brother.

The main club house was known as "the lodge." It was a large modern bungalow with a graceful sloping roof. The front of the lodge faced out over the ocean and there were floor-to-ceiling sliding glass doors. The lodge had a wide open living room with a fireplace and bookshelves, stocked mostly with books on fishing and paperback mysteries. The dining table was on one side of the living room and could seat about fourteen people, even though usually there were only half a dozen guests at any one time. On the wall by the dining table was mounted a huge, vividly colored marlin. Off the living room was a smaller room equipped as a bar, complete with bar stools and another mounted fish, a large silver bonefish.

The kitchen was situated between the living room and the bar, and it was usually a hive of activity, with the ladies singing and laughing as they cooked and washed.

The three small cabins led down from the lodge to the dock. They were simple but lovely, two separate bedrooms and bathrooms to a cabin. In time another private home was built, and further up the island an airstrip was cleared for small planes. The island was popular with fishermen and women from all over the world because it lay in the middle of very good bonefishing waters.

Bonefish are odd creatures, considered to be nearly as good sport fish as the tarpon. Like the tarpon, they are silvery white and grey and powerful swimmers. What makes the bonefish special is that it is a shallow water fish, swimming in only a few feet of water. At Deep Water Cay there was a team of about ten guides, local Bahamians who knew the waters and how to creep up silently on the feeding bonefish so they could be caught. The guide boats were equipped with outboard motors, but when bonefishing, the guide would push the boat along from the stern with a long pole. This method of propelling a boat was called poling, and it took great strength and balance.

The team of men who made up the guides included Kenneth, who was older and knew more about fishing than anyone else; Levi, who found life continually enjoyable; and Frank, Otto, Otis, David, Armand, and several others. Daddy was to manage the fishing side of the club, and it was Mommy's job to oversee the domestic side. Mommy had a team of about six to ten ladies. The head cook was a large woman called Evalina. She was wonderful to know when she was in a good mood, but I learned to steer clear of her when she was upset or angry. She had a voice that could bellow across the entire island, and most of the other people who worked with her had a healthy respect for her. Then there was Frances, a tall, slender, quiet lady, who was always sweet and kind. And Wolletta, a lively extrovert who was married to Levi; together they made an irresistible couple. There were others who were quieter or less comfortable being on friendly terms with us. Very soon Evalina and Wolletta would hug us and tease us and even tell us off gently. But the others just did their work and did not stray into the gray area of becoming friends with the boss and his family.

Mommy and Daddy took well to life on Deep Water Cay. They were immediately liked and respected by the guides and the kitchen staff as well as the guests. Mommy and Daddy instituted a short time of prayer in the kitchen each morning. The guides and the ladies took turns praying. One of the guides, Otis, had a terrible stutter, but when he prayed his stutter would disappear completely. It was quite an extraordinary phenomenon.

The Bahamians were so pleased that my parents were Christians, and that time of prayer seemed to secure their affection. Deep Water Cay offered the best jobs for miles around, and the guides and ladies were glad to be part of the operation.

The only person who caused problems was Stick, the bartender. He had been to Freeport and had lived in the city, and he was viewed by his colleagues with a certain amount of suspicion. Stick would sometimes disappear on Grand Bahama and return days later, covered in bruises and with a black eye or two. He carried a knife and was known to have used it. The problem was that he would get drunk and then pick a fight with someone. Even though he was tall and skinny (hence the nickname of "Stick"), he was wiry and strong and wild and uncontrollable when drunk. Several times a somber band of policemen had signaled to be ferried across to our island. When the policemen came over, there was great excitement, well hidden, of course. They would talk privately with Daddy with very serious faces. Sometimes Stick would be led away, glowering and muttering. Despite this, we all loved Stick and were always happy to see him again, full of life and doing his magic with the drinks behind the bar. Women especially loved Stick, and the noises behind the swing door which led into the kitchen from the dining room would always be a bit more raucous when Stick was around.

There was a special method of getting to Deep Water Cay. On the Grand Bahama side we had a flagpole which had a red flag that would be raised to indicate that someone wanted to come over. Then on our side a boat would set off, usually commanded by Daddy or Levi, to collect the guests. The system worked well, as there was always someone down by the dock to spot the red flag. We children had the run of the island, and we adored Deep Water Cay from the moment we stepped ashore. Our family was to live in the small private apartment in the main lodge. Robin and I were put out on the porch, which was fully screened so that the insects could not feast on us every night as we slept. Joel had a small elbow of a room off Mommy's and Daddy's room. We all shared one bathroom that seemed to us an unimaginable luxury: We had not had running water for four years!

Within a very short space of time, I felt more at home on Deep Water Cay than I had ever felt before. We had found a new place where we belonged, and as far as I was concerned, its name was paradise.

CHAPTER TWELVE

Ladybug and Mouser

Deep Water Cay came complete with its own dog. Ladybug was a light brindle mutt of extremely uncertain parentage. She was sweet and affectionate and seemed to take to us as much as we took to her. I do not know how many litters of pups she had had, but when we came to the island, she had just weaned a batch which were taken to the mainland to find homes. Soon after we arrived, one of the ladies brought over a small tabby kitten which she had found abandoned in Macleans Town. We were thrilled. However, the kitten was too young to be on his own and meowed piteously. Ladybug came to the rescue. She became his wet nurse. Mouser adored Ladybug, and besides feeding from her, he slept with her, played with her, and generally accepted the gentle dog as his new mother.

Ladybug always stayed close to the lodge even though she had the run of the entire island. We knew that every so often an unwanted dog would be left on the uninhabited end of Deep Water Cay to die. Sometimes the poor stranded dog would find Ladybug and the lodge and beg for food. But we did not want more than one dog, and we especially did not want any half-wild male dogs to seek out Ladybug when she was in heat.

I felt horribly sorry for these wild dogs, but even I could see that they could never become our pets. They were terrified of people and would not let any humans near them. Whenever we would come up on one scrounging in the dust bin out behind the kitchen, it would howl with fright and take off into the under-brush, disappearing to the other end of the island. In time the wild dogs would die, and the scavenging sea birds would pick their bones clean. Unless we actually saw them, we never really knew when there were any on the island.

Because of the wild dogs, Mommy always demanded that we tell her where we were going. We had to swim together and were not allowed to explore the island alone. We discovered that there were other things that went bump in the night. Once Robin and I were awakened by something moving in the palm tree right outside our screened-in porch. We were frightened enough to wake Mommy and Daddy, who came out and shone a flashlight at the tree. There, balancing precariously on a swaying palm frond, was a large, surprised-looking raccoon. It blinked at us for a moment and then scrambled quickly down the tree and lumbered off into the night. The next morning we went out and found its tracks, but we never saw the raccoon again. Of course, Robin and Joel and I wanted to entice it back and make it a pet, but Mommy and Daddy convinced us it could never be domesticated.

As Mouser grew he became an agile and playful cat, good at catching lizards and birds. But after about a year he started to display some disturbing habits. His favorite game was pounce, which we would play with him for hours on end. Sometimes he "went wild" as cats do; ears back, eyes wide, skittering around like a mad thing. One day during one of his play sessions, he went wild and pounced on Joel. He caught Joel on the shoulder and slid down his side, leaving long red welts as he went. Joel screamed and howled with the pain, and screamed even harder when Mommy dabbed on the Bactine, but he was back playing with Mouser a few hours later.

Looking back, we should have imported a female cat for Mouser, to keep him from becoming so wild. But for some reason there were no spare female cats, or perhaps we had not wanted any more cats. Perhaps some of the guests did not like animals. For whatever reason, Mouser was the sole feline inhabitant of Deep Water Cay and was becoming more and more dissatisfied with his lot. Sometimes he would vanish for days and then reappear, hungry and strange.

One afternoon as Joel was walking down the hallway to the living room, Mouser pounced on him. The cat landed on the side of Joel's face and embedded his claws into his temple, just a hair's breath from Joel's left eye. Joel screamed and the cat leapt away, hissing and growling. Mouser was definitely not behaving like our dear cat any more. He had become a dangerous stranger.

The gash by Joel's eye bled badly and turned bright pink with infection. Now even Joel was frightened of Mouser. My parents were distraught. What could be done with a cat that had gotten too wild and that jumped on people for no reason whatsoever? No one in Macleans Town wanted Mouser. They had too many hungry, half-wild cats already.

A few days after the second attack, Mommy and Daddy called us into their bedroom. They were nervous and anxious. We could sense that something horrible was going to happen. "We cannot keep Mouser any more," Mommy began, "and we cannot find a home for him. Next time he might blind one of you. We cannot take that chance." Worse, we discovered that Mouser had attacked Levi in the same way a week earlier.

We all nodded our heads silently. Then Daddy cleared his

throat. "I'm afraid we will have to do away with Mouser." Instantly his words were drowned out by our cries of "No! No! You can't kill Mouser. You can't." Joel sobbed the hardest of all, " No, no, don't kill Mouser, he'll be all right. I know he won't do it again." But we all knew that he might, and Mommy and Daddy had made up their minds. We went and found Mouser where he was sleeping peacefully and each of us said good-bye to him, weeping as we did so. Then Mommy took us children out of the lodge, and with aching hearts, we walked down to the beach.

Daddy was left to do the dirty work. He picked up Mouser, slipped him quickly into a pillowcase, and tied the opening with a bit of rope. Then he took the howling, writhing cat down to the mud flats, which were on the opposite side of the island to the beach. There he placed the pillowcase on the mud and walked back from it. Then, with one bullet from a rifle, he shot Mouser dead.

Over on the beach we heard the shot and burst into a fresh chorus of sobbing. Mommy was crying too. Daddy buried Mouser in a place we had chosen, because he did not want us to see Mouser dead and shot. Our whole family was in mourning, and we children kept freshly picked flowers on the grave.

One consequence which could not have been foreseen was Robin's and Joel's and my reaction to Daddy. He had decided to shoot Mouser rather than drown him, because he said it would be quicker. At the time, we had accepted that. But after Mouser's death, we three felt a chilling fear of Daddy and a strange loathing for him. We spoke of our feelings to each other, and realized we were all feeling the same. To us Daddy was now a man who could deliberately shoot a cat dead. None of us could bear to think of him taking aim and firing at the wriggling, yowling pillowcase. "He did it because he loves us more than a cat," said Robin, the voice of reason. "But Mouser was our pet," insisted Joel, who felt somewhat to blame.

The only option had been to take Mouser to the mainland and set him loose there. But Mommy and Daddy had pointed out that he would probably have been eaten by a wild dog, and none of us wanted that. In our heads we could not come to terms with what had happened, but neither could we think of anything else that we could have done.

What made it worse was knowing that it wasn't really anybody's fault. It was a sad situation for which there had been no easy answer, no acceptable answer. We thought back to Tammy and Cabin Boy, and our grief and perplexity deepened.

Luckily, within a week, our fear and distaste for Daddy went away. One by one we laid to rest our anger and our hurt. I tried not to think about Mouser being shot, but when I did I focused on a thought: "Mouser might have blinded someone." It was better to blame the cat than anyone or anything else. In time our heaviness lifted and our grief subsided, and it was a genuine relief to no longer have the threat of another attack.

A little while after that Ladybug disappeared. When she had been gone for a few days, we started to worry about her. Usually she stayed close by, and whenever she did roam, she always came back after a day or two, wagging her tail, licking our faces, and covered with prickles. But this time she did not come back. Mommy went out on a long walk and called for her. Daddy walked up and down the island and called for her. We were now very worried. Half looking for Ladybug, half just exploring, I took a walk to the end of the island, to the places where we were not really supposed to go alone. But I went, hunting for shells, listening to the birds, and looking for Ladybug.

I found her toward the wild end of the island under a bush just off a sandy path. She was bloated grotesquely, and flies were buzzing around her. I ran all the way back to the lodge and told the rest of the family. The only slight consolation in finding Ladybug dead was that it was I who had found her. I had succeeded in finding her even after grownups had tried and failed. I felt a bond with Ladybug in her death. She had let me find her, and that was special, a privilege. She had made Mommy and Daddy proud of me and Robin and Joel somewhat envious of me. I had been brave enough to hunt for her in the wild places, and my bravery had been rewarded. We buried Ladybug next to Mouser, and this time we were all involved. Although very sad, it was not a painful burial.

We discovered that Ladybug had eaten the poisonous innards of a fish which she had pilfered from the kitchen scrap bucket. The Bahamians ate certain types of fish which we considered dubious, if not downright poisonous. The day Ladybug had disappeared, the ladies in the kitchen had cooked one such fish. Ladybug had probably sneaked the discarded entrails and died of the poison.

Everyone missed Ladybug, with her gentle smile and her constant affection, and the island felt strange without any animals. A few weeks later one of the ladies arrived on the island with a small frisky puppy, a cross between a boxer and a mongrel. She had eyes rimmed with black markings that made her look like Cleopatra, a white bib, and a caramel coat. We called her Cocoplum. Her energy and "puppyness" made us laugh, and we let

Ladybug rest in peace.

When it came time for us to leave Deep Water Cay, Cocoplum was there to say goodbye to us. She stayed on as the island's dog, loved and pampered by guests and staff alike. But while we lived with her, Cocoplum made up for the sadness of Mouser and Ladybug and kept us children happy and busy, throwing sticks for her, playing tag, and even taking her swimming with us.

The *Tappan Zee.*

I plot our progress with a compass.

On deck, protected by a safety net, as
we sail down the Intracoastal Waterway.

I'm swinging in the bosun's
chair as we sail down the
Intracoastal waterway.

The *Tappan Zee* moored at Boca Raton.

Cabin Boy.

Upper right: Weaving palm fronds, with Cocoplum watching.

Lower right: Studying, at Deep Water Cay.

Joel with a bonefish he caught.

Nighttime at
Deep Water Cay

April Fools day. In the costume I fooled my father with.

Peter Klopman, with me on the left, Robin on the right.

Here I'm entering the small amphibian plane to fly to Florida from Deep Water Cay all by myself.

CHAPTER THIRTEEN

Minnow

The coastline of Deep Water Cay which faced Grand Bahama was made up of the tangled roots and branches of mangrove trees growing in the mud flats. This stretch was where the bonefish lived and fed. Because the water was so shallow and so full of small fish, sea plants, and living shells, it was a haven for birds as well.

Great blue and great white herons would wade for hours on end, at times standing motionless like garden statues, at times chasing a prey and jabbing at it with their long beaks. Besides the great white and great blue herons, there were the smaller white herons, green herons, and tricolored herons. The tricolored herons were dark green and brown birds, with the distinctive heron shape but with a slightly shorter neck and legs. Sometimes they had paler stripes on their heads and mottled markings on their breasts.

There were also the energetic kingfishers, who would dive tirelessly after their prey. Once in a while we would spot a hawk. Occasionally, even the striking man-of-war birds would descend from their high currents of air to come and roost in the mangroves. Mangroves are wonderful trees which need to live half in the water. Their roots protrude from the underside of the pliant, smooth branches and grow downwards into the water until they finally secure themselves in the muddy soil of the bottom.

There were snails and other shells which preferred the calmer mud flats to the pounding freshness of the ocean side. Besides the bonefish, there were languid needlefish with their long, thin snouts and iridescent bodies and the small sergeant-majors with their bright black and yellow stripes. There were mullets, large grey fish which swim in huge schools, and many, many other varieties. Last, but certainly not least, were the minnows. These small fish, usually no longer than a child's thumb, would swim in vast schools that must have numbered into the hundreds of thousands. Sometimes a larger fish would threaten a school, and the myriads of tiny fish would leap out of the water to escape. At these times the water looked as if it was being rained on with hundreds of silver droplets.

Every so often I would put on an old pair of canvas shoes and go wading in the mud flats, hoping for a new shell or a glimpse of something special. One day I waded out beyond the back garden of the lodge, which sloped down to the flats. These were separated only by a short sturdy wall which had been built to keep the water from flooding the coarse grass of the garden. In bad storms the water would come over the wall, but under normal conditions the wall was an effective barrier.

Not far out I noticed some small animal or bird flopping under a mangrove tree. I went to investigate and found a young tricolored heron entangled in the network of roots. I bent down and spoke soothingly to the small bird, hoping I would not send it further into the snarled roots or deeper into the water. But it sat there and stared up at me, panting with its exertions. I called to it again and it took a few crooked, unsteady steps toward me. I held out my hand, beckoning it, and cooing softly. The bedraggled bird flopped its way over to me and out from under the roots of the mangrove. "Where is your nest?" I asked it, but it just opened its beak and looked up at me. I looked around hoping to see an adult tricolored heron watching somewhere in the distance, but I saw no heron. The small bird squeaked at me. It was hungry. Not knowing what else to do, I gently scooped the bird up into my arms and waded back to the garden and into the lodge.

The heron was instantly popular. The rest of the family could hardly believe I had actually found it stranded and in need of help. Mommy and Daddy examined the bird, but could find nothing wrong with it, no injury. It was just a small tricolored heron who had strayed too far from its nest and gotten lost.

The poor bird was very hungry and began to squawk loudly for some food. We did not know what tricolored herons ate but decided it must be the small fish which swarm over the flats. Daddy dug out a large seining net about the size of a tennis net, only broader, with holes small enough to catch tiny fish. Robin and Joel and I went seining, one of us holding the bird while the other two held the ends of the net. In our first catch we got about one hundred minnows. We brought them and the heron onto the grass and put the bird down onto the opened net full of tiny flapping fish. Its reaction was impressive. Immediately it speared a fish with its beak and swallowed it whole. Again and again it stabbed at the minnows, eating them eagerly and quickly. The heron ate almost all the minnows we had caught. Then it lost interest in the fish and walked unsteadily off the net. If it had had chops it would have licked them. We were delighted. At last we had found a way to keep the bird alive. Because it had been so happy with the minnows, we named the heron "Minnow," and even though we were not certain, we declared that Minnow was a "he."

Minnow seemed content to live with us and became very attentive. We fixed a night shelter for him where he could rest and sleep. Every morning we would gather up the net and catch Minnow some breakfast. We learned that one meal a day was not enough for him. We seined twice a day and then three times. That seemed to suit Minnow, so we fed him three times a day, about one hundred live minnows at each meal. Minnow grew and became more elegant and heron-like. His walk became more graceful and sure-footed, even though he still squawked at us and demanded his fish loudly. While we seined, Minnow liked to stand on the short wall looking out over the flats and watch our progress. Often he would hop down and take a stab at a small fish swimming by. But he could not catch enough for his huge appetite, and he preferred to wander around the garden with us rather than spend his days wading the way a heron should.

Once in a while we caught sight of some adult tricolored herons, perched silently on nearby mangrove trees, but Minnow took no notice of them. Instead, he filled his days with standing on the wall, walking in the garden, eating, playing with us, and watching us fish. He liked being stroked and held, and he would peck at us playfully with his long beak.

Minnow had been with us a few months when we began to notice some changes. More and more he liked to stand on the wall and wade out into the flats by himself. He was getting better at fishing and would supplement our catches with fish of his own. He continued to grow taller and larger, and his feathers took on a deep shine. Occasionally, instead of striding elegantly over to us when we came to him, he would edge away and stand aloof. We realized that he must be returned to the wild. We carried on fishing for him, but less and less, telling him that he must catch his own. The play stopped, quite naturally. Suddenly he did not want to have us hold him and stroke him any more. In the mornings when we would race down to see him and catch him breakfast, he would already be wading in the water as if to say, "Thank you very much all the same, but I am quite able to manage on my own." After a while the net lay in a heap under the kitchen steps, unused and unneeded.

The day came when Minnow wandered off and did not come back in the evening. We were worried that he had been caught by a raccoon or a shark. But the next day Minnow was back, standing serenely in the water, fishing. We were as proud of him as we were sorry to lose him, but we all knew that this was the better way. Sometimes Robin and Joel and I would sit on the wall and look for Minnow, calling out his name. And then a handsome tricolored heron would swoop down and land not far from us, giving us a brief backwards glance before turning away to fish.

Minnow must have settled in the mangroves not far from us, because we spotted him off and on until we left Deep Water Cay. He seemed to have made a full transition back into the wild, because sometimes he was accompanied by another heron. If ever we looked out over the flats and saw a tricolored heron standing close in to the shore, we could almost be certain it was Minnow. He may have gone back to the wild, but he had not forgotten a place where the fishing was uncommonly good.

CHAPTER FOURTEEN

Fishing and Shelling

After the initial excitement and upheaval of coming to Deep
Water Cay, we children had settled into a daily routine. I doubt
that we would have settled into that particular routine if left to
ourselves, but as it was, we were not left to ourselves. Mommy
organized time for study, complete with homework, spelling tests,
and other scholarly activities. She sent away for correspondence
courses for us, each according to our own particular grade.
Mommy chose the Calvert Correspondence Course, which
operated from Baltimore, Maryland. Our syllabuses and textbooks
arrived in several boxes through the post, and were collected from
the post office in Freeport on one of Daddy's trips there for
provisions. It was an exciting moment, opening the battered
cardboard boxes and pulling out book after book, each one brand
new and crisp. It was like getting a magic present, and we couldn't
wait to dive into our studies.

I can remember my syllabus, which had a silhouette of a boy
with thick wavy hair and a slight overbite on the cover. Every day I
would open it and turn to the section for that day. There I would
read what I was supposed to accomplish in each of the separate
subjects: spelling, math, history, English, science, writing, and
reading. I found the work easy and would often do much more
than the daily allotment. We all discovered that if we worked
steadily from about nine o'clock until twelve noon, we could finish
an entire day's lesson and possibly more. Mommy saw no reason
to make us work a bit in the morning and a bit after lunch, so we
did our whole day's work in the morning. By lunch time we were
free for the rest of the day. If it was hot and sunny, we would swim
and play on the beach. If Mommy needed some fish for the
evening meal, then we would fish.

By now Robin and Joel and I could be relied upon to catch
and clean enough fish for the guests as well as for ourselves. I
loved to fish, particularly from the dock, where we would squat
alongside the *Tappan Zee* and lower our simple drop lines into the
water. The water was so clear that we could see straight to the
bottom, which was about twelve feet below the surface. We would
come equipped with a bucket for the fish and a few good knives.
First we would catch one fish with a scrap from the kitchen. Then
we would cut up the first fish we caught, unless it was particularly

large or special in any way, and use it as bait to catch all the rest.

One day I remember Mommy telling me she was planning grilled fish for that evening. We had about ten guests, almost the maximum number the club could accommodate. After lunch Mommy sent me off to the dock, bucket and drop line in hand. It was a particularly clear day without a breeze in the sky. No breeze meant that the water would be especially clear, the surface undisturbed. I caught the first fish almost immediately, a small grunt. Grunts are good-tasting fish with beautiful yellow and turquoise stripes covering their bodies. Grunts were biting that day, and I hauled them in one after the other. I caught a few snappers as well, a pinkish and grey fish which has, some would say, the sweetest tasting flesh of all. After I had caught enough for each guest to have two or three and for us to have the same amount, I set to work cleaning the fish. Scrape, scrape, off came the scales. Slish-slash, off came the heads, out came the innards, over and over, until I was finished. That day I timed myself; I had caught and cleaned thirty fish in about one and a quarter hours.

The fish did not always throw themselves onto my hook the way they did that day, but fishing off the dock at Deep Water Cay was usually a rewarding experience. Sometimes one of the guests would grow tired of trying for the wily and elusive bonefish and wind up with a drop line at the end of the dock. It was not sport fishing, and it took no special talent or strength, but it was fun!

Once when I was walking under the dock on the beach, I noticed a school of puffer fish swimming very near the shore. Almost without thinking, I lunged into the school and came up with an irate puffer struggling in my fist. It seemed so outraged at being grabbed out of the water that it sank its powerful parrotlike jaw into the palm of my hand. I screamed and dropped it immediately. It darted back into deeper water to rejoin the school which had dispersed wildly when I had attacked. My hand was bleeding, and there was a loose V-shaped flap of skin where the fish had bitten me. I ran back up to the lodge, dabbed on the Bactine, and stuck on the Band Aid. I was terribly proud of my cut and later of the scar and would explain when asked, "Oh, that's where the puffer fish bit me when I caught it with my bare hands."

Another proud time came when Daddy said that I was strong enough to go out for a bonefish. One of the guides was assigned to me, and off we went in our own boat. The guide, I believe it was Kenneth, poled strongly and silently over the flats, all the while keeping a lookout for any sign of a bonefish. I looked as well, scanning the surface of the water for a telltale fin or even a ripple. Kenneth spotted a fish feeding in the shallow water just below the surface. "Cast at one o'clock," he whispered to me excitedly.

That meant I was to cast my line just to the right of the bow. That method of giving directions was very useful when bonefishing, when even the merest movement could send the fish speeding away. Besides being an accurate way of defining direction, it did not require visual contact with the guide. I could keep staring out over the water and attending to my line while being told exactly where to cast. To understand the directions, I only needed to imagine the face of a large clock lying upwards in front of the boat, the bow corresponding to twelve o'clock. Anyone who can tell time can follow the directions.

I cast my line, but it fell short and the fish vanished. We poled on, the only sound the dripping of water as the pole was pulled out and pushed in over and over. Kenneth spotted another bonefish. "Cast at nine o'clock," he whispered to me. Again I cast, and again the fish saw me coming. Nothing. I reeled in the line and waited. We ghosted silently over the flats for hours, baking in the intense heat. I had on my sunglasses to help cut through the glare on the water and a straw hat to keep from getting a headache. I was wearing a zip-up play suit, combining shorts and a sleeveless blouse. It was yellow and white seersucker, and I had thought it would be cool enough for the day. But under that sun I dripped with sweat, and it stuck to my body like a wet handkerchief. Kenneth had on long trousers and a ragged T-shirt. He too was streaming with sweat. After several fruitless hours we paused for lunch. Mommy had packed sandwiches and a cool drink. It is absolutely true that fishing gives one a fearsome appetite, but then I was always hungry, whether or not I was fishing.

After lunch, Kenneth took up the pole again, and we turned for home, still on the lookout for bonefish. We spotted a few and I made a few casts, but no luck. I was beginning to feel a little discouraged with bonefishing. "What's so great about this," I thought to myself, "when I could be on the dock catching as many fish as I like?" All of a sudden Kenneth whispered another o'clock and I cast. This time a fish took my line. I let it run, as I had been taught to do, and when the whizzing, unwinding line had slowed a little, I started to wind in gently to see what type of fish I had hooked. Instantly the fish was off again, even with that lightest of tugs. The line sang out again from the reel, and I watched it unwind as if by magic. Again it slowed. Again I slowly started to wind up the line. Far away from the boat, a bonefish jumped high into the air and splashed down again. That was my fish! Kenneth was delighted and gave me a constant stream of advice. "Pull it in now . . . let it go . . . take in that slack . . . !"

I gripped the pole and played the fish, first letting it run and then pulling it in. Several times it leaped out of the water. It was immensely strong. I could not believe that a creature less than two feet in length could give such a fight. I was beginning to understand why people liked to sport-fish. It was completely different from my drop line on the end of the dock. I felt as if I were pitting not only my muscles but also my wits against those of the fish, and so far, it was an even draw.

But a bonefish, especially a smallish bonefish, is no match for a well placed hook and a strong line. After a while the constant pulling grew less insistent. I was able to wind up much of the line that earlier had sped through my fingers. The fish was beginning to tire. Bit by bit I reeled in the line until Kenneth and I could see the shimmering darting strip of silver on the end of it. As we were over shallow water and a white sandy bottom, Kenneth suggested that I hop out of the boat and land the fish from the water. It felt wonderful to slip up to my waist into the water. Even though the water was warm, it felt mercifully cooler than the unremitting heat. We were now close enough to the dock for people on the island to have spotted us. Daddy came over in another boat, a broad grin on his face. When I had reeled in the bonefish close to the boat, Kenneth scooped it up in a net and undid the hook which was embedded in the side of its mouth. Kenneth let me look at the fish, and I stroked its glistening side before he lowered it gently back into the water.

The fish was exhausted and swam off slowly and unsteadily as if in a daze. We could see it make its way back over the flat, gradually getting faster, until at last it blended with the shining sunlight on the water and disappeared. Daddy was so proud of me that he took a picture of me standing nearly up to my waist in the water holding the pole. I had caught a bonefish! It was as if I had been put through some primitive initiation rite, and passed. I was nine years old.

There was something else I loved doing even more than fishing, however--shelling. I suppose I thought swimming to be the very best thing in the world, and when it could be combined with shelling, as it often was, then paradise really did exist on earth. Deep Water Cay was an excellent place for shells. On the ocean side the island sloped off gently, with a long white sand bar stretching out for about a quarter of a mile when the tide was out. The day after a storm was an especially good time to look for shells. Sometimes the wind and waves would toss up heavier shells or more unusual specimens. Ordinarily the pale sands would be covered at the tide line with a wide band of smaller shells, but after a storm all sorts of interesting flotsam and jetsam would appear.

There was the common, but no less lovely for that, sunrise talon, a thin polished bivalve painted delicate rays of pinks and yellows, just like a sunrise. There were the tiny, plump coffee bean shells, the wiggly worm shells, the smooth, glossy olive shells, the cone, fig, tulip, limpet, tun, scallop, triton, conch, clam, bleeding teeth; and so many, many more. One of my favorites was the murex, a graceful univalve with lacy-looking flutes running down its back. We tried to learn all the proper names of the shells we found. We had a shell book with which we identified any new varieties. We even learned the Latin names so we could distinguish them more accurately. I cannot remember many of the Latin names now, but they used to be part of our shell language.

Some shells intrigued me because of their color, some because of their shape or their shininess or their size, and some because of how they had to be collected. Two shells in particular were special because of the methods needed to collect them: the flamingo tongue and the goldshell.

The flamingo tongue is a small univalve only about an inch or so in length. There are several varieties of flamingo tongue, but the one I knew best was the leopard-spotted flamingo tongue. To find the shell alive, it was necessary to dive for it. It grows on the sea fans and sea fronds on teeming coral reefs in the tropics. We had a beautiful reef right off Deep Water Cay out beyond the sand bar. There was an abundance of sea fans and fronds, swaying plants covered with tiny crustacea in unbelievably bright yellow and purple. They looked as if they had been dipped in thick paint. There were the sea anemones, flowerlike creatures that trap and sting unsuspecting fish and shellfish. These were glowing red, muted mauve, deep gold, and many other beautiful shades. Sometimes they struck up symbiotic relationships with certain types of fish, who would feed on their debris. It was not uncommon to see a vibratingly bright, tiny fish hovering in the arms of a sea anemone. The colors and intensity of the fish and sea plants always had a strange effect on me. There was something so beautiful, outlandish, and improbable about the reefs that filled me with an intense elation, a wild joy, a sense of euphoria. Our times snorkeling over the reefs were like experiencing an entirely new world, more wonderful and fantastic than one could have ever imagined.

Skin diving was a special ritual. I can remember the excitement of dipping my flippers into the water to make them easy to pull on and then spitting into my mask so that it would not fog up so quickly, pulling that into place, and lastly, adjusting the snorkel. The final act of biting down on the mouthpiece of the snorkel to secure it in my mouth was the signal for an adventure to begin. As I submerged, all the sounds of the land and sky would be drowned out by the sound of the water closing around me and the sound of my own breathing. I suppose it was like going back into the womb and becoming weightless, and above all, free.

The sense of freedom I felt under water was immense. No matter what had happened on land that day, a good long swim would, if not make it come right, at least make it go away and alter my perspective. Perhaps some psychiatrists do send certain patients off for skin diving in the tropics. If they don't, they should. I think the benefits of snorkeling over a reef for a month might outweigh the benefits of lying on a hard couch in a strange room off and on for years. I know which I would prefer.

Added to the emotional high were the visual delights and the simple but exquisite pleasure of moving through the water. Some days we would spend up to eight hours in the water, and it was rare if we did not go swimming even briefly, at least once or twice a day. The motivation to do my studies quickly, even though I loved them, was very strong indeed. Mommy let us swim from the beach and dive from the dock by ourselves, but Mommy or Daddy always accompanied us when we went skin diving over the reefs.

I believe we had heard about flamingo tongues but had never found a live one ourselves until we came to Deep Water Cay. One day we were swimming over the reef when one of us spotted a strange lump on a sea fan. The small shape was covered with leopard skin. The sea fans were growing about six feet under water, and we all swam down to them to examine the odd creatures. We had been taught not to touch or disturb strange objects we saw under water, for our own protection as well as for the sake of the object. However, one of us risked a prod, and lo and behold, the leopard mantle disappeared and revealed a shiny peach-colored shell. We at once recognized the flamingo tongue and picked it off the fan. The leopard skin was part of the animal's body which could be retracted into the shell and used as camouflage. The mottled, spotted shape was certainly less likely to be seen and eaten than a bright clearly defined shell.

Collecting flamingo shells was like hunting for miniature baby leopards in an undersea jungle. Often we would dive and not see even one flamingo tongue. At other times we would come upon a whole colony of the shells. From then on we always kept an eye out for flamingo tongues.

The other shell that was a special challenge to find was the goldshell. Goldshells are tiny droplets of shells shaped like bright golden tears. They were highly prized by the Bahamians who would sell them by the bucketful to traders. The shells would then be made into jewelery and sold to tourists, usually in Nassau or Freeport. Goldshells are carnivorous creatures and they live buried in the mud flats. Apart from digging up and sieving an entire mud flat, which would be entirely unrealistic, there was only one way to catch the shells, and that was to entice them up to the surface of the mud with small chunks of meat.

It was a messy business, and we always went goldshelling with some of the guides. First one of the guides would choose a section of mud which had to be stirred up by walking around in it. When the mud was well roiled, we would throw small chunks of fish or meat onto the top of it. And then we would wait. It was sometimes as long as half an hour before the first minute specks of gold could be seen making their way toward a piece of meat. The little creatures were crafty. If we waded back into the mud too soon, they would sense danger and vanish back into the mud, and that would be the end of that. They did not like the smell of people. We would have to wash our legs and feet very thoroughly to disguise our scent. Because it required wading knee deep in mud, we always wore our bathing suits and went barefoot. For those people who like wallowing in glorious mud, it was the ideal outing--and I was one of those people. There was something indescribably luscious about wading around in the dark, squelchy ooze.

We would wait patiently for the shells to smell the bait and come to the surface. It was best to wait until the creatures had actually got to a piece of meat and started to eat it. Once they started to feed, they seemed to become much less concerned about the large legs wading around them. When each piece of meat had a cluster of goldshells around it and when the mud was dotted with other aroused shells, it was time for the catch. This was the part I liked best. It was important to act as quickly and calmly as possible.

I would slide smoothly into the mud, holding a bucket over my left arm. With my right arm I would bend over and swiftly pick up the shells one by one. Often I could feel the shells between my toes, and I would grip my toes around them and bring them up to the surface. After about an hour we would have collected all the shells. Then it was back home to rinse off the shells and leave them to soak. In a few days the animals would die and float out of the shells. They were then ready to sell, or in our case, add to our shell collection. It was good of the guides to let us children come, because every shell we collected was one less for them, and they sold the shells to help feed their families.

We children each had our own individual shell collections, which were guarded and tended as if they were hoards of jewels. Even though I now appreciate the difference between a diamond and a conch, I still treasure my shells. They are incomparable works of art, ingeniously designed and crafted, exquisitely painted and beautifully finished.

I kept my smaller shells in plastic fishing tackle boxes which had lots of tiny drawers. I kept my miniature shells wrapped in toilet paper or cotton wool. These I hunted on my hands and knees on the beaches. I would choose a tide mark that stretched down the beach and then I would crawl over it, a container beside me. That was the only way to find really small shells, because even from my height as a child when standing, it was impossible to make out the perfect miniature shells from the other bits of broken shells and coral.

I also collected large shells, and these I displayed on the top of my dresser or on a window ledge. I had a prize trumpet triton, the type of shell blown by characters from ancient mythology. Tritons have a long spiral which swells to a curve at the opening and then gradually tapers to the other end. I had to dive for my triton which was still alive when I found it. I also had a large helmet shell, thick and rounded on the back with a flat polished face. I had several beautiful pink and white queen conches, the ubiquitous emblem of the Bahamas.

Besides these shells, I had gathered branches of staghorn coral, so named because it resembles the antlers of a deer. I had sturdy clumps of brain coral, which, as its name suggests, looks like brains. I had starfish, large and small. The smaller ones were usually found in the shallow water or washed up on the beach already dead. The larger ones I had to dive for. When alive, starfish are heavy and can be prickly. I had to ask one of the guides to clean all my large starfish, because I could not even cut through their skin.

I also collected sea urchins, which I preferred dead to alive. Their skeletons are fragile and beautiful bun-shaped objects. Alive they are spiny and prickly menaces. From time to time one of us would step on a sea urchin. If it was a small bristly one, no harm would be done. It felt rather like stepping on the top of a stiff broom. But if one of us stepped on a long-spined sea urchin, it was another matter. The spines were as sharp as needles and could even pierce through our flippers. The prickles hurt like fire, and even though it was painful, we would try to pull out the spines immediately. Sometimes they came out cleanly, but sometimes they broke off, and the poor victim would hobble around for days with a throbbing foot until the spine worked itself to the surface.

Besides the long-spined sea urchins, there were other creatures we had to watch out for underwater. There was stinging coral, which if brushed against would make the skin feel as if it were on fire. There were some nasty anemones which could sting. Some of the innocent-looking sea plumes and grasses could sting as well. Occasionally we came across the brilliant blue bubbles and trailing tentacles of the Portuguese Man-of-War jellyfish. Happily, these were rare. Apart from the really dangerous creatures like sharks or the deadly sea snake, which we saw only once, there were bad-tempered biters like the moray eel, the barracuda, and many other lesser nuisances. We became adept at identifying, and in most cases, avoiding danger. Perhaps more importantly, we learned how to live with it. In the midst of all this beauty and danger, collecting shells was one of the safer and more satisfying things to do!

CHAPTER FIFTEEN

Yacht Magic to the Rescue

There was a certain routine that went on every morning on Deep Water Cay, and it involved Daddy in a minor form of deception. Most boats and yachts are equipped with a device called a ship-to-shore radio. This is like a grown-up, long distance walkie-talkie, and only boats were allowed to have them. Since we were actually living in the lodge and not on a boat, we should not have had a ship-to-shore radio, but we did. It was necessary for Daddy to communicate with the yachts that were coming to visit the island and also for him to communicate with passing yachts, as well as receive messages from the Coast Guard or other people who might have something important or even urgent to tell him. The ship-to-shore radio was hidden in Daddy's office in the lodge, and its code name was "Yacht Magic." The owner of the island had a yacht called *Magic*, which he sometimes kept at the dock or sometimes back at his home in Florida, but the radio always stayed in Daddy's office. When other people called for "Yacht Magic," they assumed they were talking to someone aboard a yacht, that is, unless they knew the set-up.

One morning when Daddy was listening to the ship-to-shore radio, he heard through the crackle and the static a frantic lady's voice calling "SOS, SOS." SOS is the internationally agreed code for "Help," and the letters stand for "Save our ship." If anyone hears an "SOS" call, they are duty bound to help if they can, or to get someone else to help. So, of course, the moment Daddy heard the lady calling "SOS," he knew he had to help her somehow. He stayed listening to the radio, hoping she would give out her position and more information about what was happening to her. In a moment Daddy heard her voice again, and this time she was sobbing and saying, "We are lost and stranded," but she still did not say where she was.

After a few minutes of Daddy straining to hear the lady, he suddenly heard a man's voice. "This is the United States Coast Guard," it said, "we are receiving you. Where are you located?" There was a bit of crackle and then the lady came on again, moaning, "I don't know, somewhere in the Bahamas, near Grand Bahama, I think. Help me, help me." The Coast Guard man tried again. "What is the name of your yacht?" he asked her. More crackle and then the lady answered, "I'm on the *Sylva*. We've come from Miami." The Coast Guard asked her if there was water in the bilge.

The bilge is the part of a boat that is under the water line and under the floorboards, so most people never see a bilge unless they wish to or have to. But checking the bilge for water is one of the best ways of telling whether a boat is sinking, that is, if you can't tell in some other, more obvious way. Most bilges are rather foul places, filled with dirt, grease, and great hunks of metal called ballast. Ballast is what is needed to help keep a boat upright and sitting in the water properly. On the *Tappan Zee* we had dozens of small lead bricks known as "lead pigs." I don't know why they were called pigs, but whenever we had to move them we got as dirty as pigs. Once in a while we would have a bilge-cleaning day, and Daddy would take up all the floor boards and haul out the lead bars which would be covered in a putrid, filthy, greasy slime. Then we would dig around in the bilge, discovering objects that we had lost or dropped by accident. Daddy would scrape out the worst of the muck, while Mommy, Robin, Joel, and I would scrub and wash the pigs. It was an unsavory task, and I can remember actually getting sick on at least one bilge-excavating operation.

But back to the lady on the *Sylva*. There was a moment of silence, and then she answered that she didn't know whether or not there was water in the bilge but that she did know the boat was aground. The Coast Guard then asked, "How deep is the water around you?" The lady said, "Wait a minute. I'll check with the broom handle." Silence again, then the lady came on and said, "The water is up to here." The Coast Guard man was beginning to find this conversation a bit hard going. Very patiently, but with an edge of exasperation in his voice, he asked her, "Could you tell me how deep is 'up to here?'" There was more crackling before the lady came on with the answer, "It's just above my waist."

This was good news, because at least the water was so shallow that the boat was not going to sink. The Coast Guard then started talking to the Bahamian police, who had just come on the line, and they handed over the problem to the police with impolite haste.

By this time the lady was almost hysterical. She kept on screaming for help and also started blabbering something about two men. "What men?" asked the new voice of the police officer. "The two men with me," the lady managed to say. "They've left me. They've jumped overboard, and now they're trying to make it to the shore. One of them has a knife". Then her voice trailed off into incoherent weeping and moaning.

The plot was thickening; now it involved two men and a knife as well as the yacht which had run aground and the hysterical lady.

Maybe the men were pirates who had kidnapped the lady! Of course by now, Daddy's office was crammed full with all of us straining to hear every word, determined not to miss any of the excitement. Daddy must have announced his presence on the line, because the next thing we heard was the police speaking to "Yacht Magic." "Yacht Magic here," Daddy replied. "Where are you located?" asked the police voice. Daddy told him our location, which was off the tip of the east coast of Grand Bahama. Daddy was not afraid of getting into trouble with the police for having the radio on land, because he had worked out a sensible explanation just in case. He would say absolutely truthfully that "Yacht Magic" was the call sign for the *Magic*, but since we were living on Deep Water Cay, with the boat at the dock, we had brought the radio onto shore to be able to use it conveniently. Whether he ever had to use that explanation or not I don't remember, but he never got into trouble for having the radio on land.

Daddy told the police that he had lots of small boats and several men available and that he would be happy to help out in any way he could. The policeman then asked him to send a boat across to the mainland to pick up a policeman and a constable who would drive from Freeport to the dock across from Deep Water Cay on Grand Bahama. Daddy thought he'd better send two boats, so the police would not be crowded. Kenneth and Otto set off in one boat, and Obert and Armand went in another to be ready to bring the police over to Deep Water Cay. In the meantime the police kept the lady talking on the radio, even though she was not really making sense any more.

The police arrived in an hour or so, and they were brought over to Deep Water Cay by the eager guides. Daddy went down to the dock to greet them, and we all followed behind him. The police were armed and looked very serious indeed. Robin and Joel and I lurked behind some sea grape bushes so we could hear what was being said without being in the way. One of the policemen looked at his watch, and we heard him say, "The plane will be here soon." As if on cue, we saw and heard the small seaplane coming into our harbor. It landed on the water a way out from the dock, and the policemen, who had got back into the small boats, were taken out to the plane. The police and Kenneth, the most senior guide, climbed into the plane, and the remaining guides sped their boats back to the dock. The plane turned around so it was facing out to sea, revved up its engine, and took off again.

Because the lady did not know where she was, it had been decided to look for the *Sylva* by air. Now all we could do was wait by the radio for news of how the search was progressing. We raced back up to the lodge and once again piled into Daddy's office. The lady was still on the line, but by now she was just weeping and sniffing and not saying much. We could hear the police talking to her and trying to keep her calm.

Several hours went by. Robin and Joel and I abandoned our eavesdropping and went to swim and play by the dock. We were a bit confused about what was going on anyway, and after the police and Kenneth had flown away, there was nothing to do or see--and we had certainly heard enough of the helpless lady.

It was late afternoon before Daddy came down to the dock with the exciting news that the police had found the boat and were bringing it back to Deep Water Cay. Another hour or so went by before we suddenly saw a large fishing boat coming into view and heading straight for us. As the boat got closer we could see Kenneth at the helm, proudly steering it to our dock. It was a typical deep-sea fishing boat, built to survive the rolling swells of the Atlantic. It had a tall upper cabin that was nearly all glassed in, so in the event of bad weather, the people fishing could still see where they were going. On top of that was the helm, where Kenneth now stood with a noble expression on his face. The *Sylva* also had great painted fish along its wooden railings. She was definitely a boat for the tourist trade, not for the professional fisherman.

Kenneth brought her expertly up to the dock where she was made fast, and the engine was turned off. By this time the dock was lined with everyone who was on the island that day, the rest of the guides, the cooks, and all of us. Kenneth jumped off the *Sylva* onto the dock, followed by the policeman, and then came the constable supporting the lady. She was helped down onto the dock where she stood like a lost sheep. We stared at her unashamedly. She had the look of someone who had awakened into one of her own nightmares. Her shoulder-length, wavy, brown hair was disheveled and flattened, and her face was streaked with tears and old make-up. She looked ill as well as upset, and when she stood on the dock she could not stand up straight. She leaned against the constable as if he was supporting her very being. She had on a light, flimsy blouse with some inappropriately bright flowers on it, a pastel skirt, and a pair of high-heeled sandals. She looked so pathetic and woebegone that I felt sorry for her.

There was much talking between the officers and Daddy, and then things started to happen. The policeman got into one of the small boats and was ferried back to the mainland, where his car and another police car were waiting for him. The seaplane droned into view and once again landed on the water near our dock. The constable and the lady then got into a small boat, and one of the guides took them out to the plane. They climbed into the plane, and the guide returned to the dock. We could see the small boat which had taken the policeman to the mainland returning with three people in it. Instead of coming to our dock, it went straight to the plane. We could see another policeman and two scruffy men get into the plane. The two escaped men had been picked up by the police! Then the boat came back to us. The plane immediately turned toward the open sea and took off.

After this flurry of activity, only our family and the cooks and guides were left, and the *Sylva*, of course, which rubbed and creaked wearily against the dock. "What happened, Daddy?" we shouted. "Tell us what happened." We had had to stand and wait and watch for so long that now we could hardly contain ourselves. Daddy, with Kenneth's help, filled in the story for their eager audience.

In Miami the night before, the lady, a friend of hers, and one of the *Sylva*'s crew had gone out for a drink. They had all gotten drunk and in the dead of the night, they had had the wonderful idea of taking the *Sylva* out for a little ride. So the three of them had piled aboard the *Sylva* and headed her out into the ocean in the pitch dark.

The next thing any of them remembered was waking up aground somewhere in the Bahamas. The two men were terrified of getting into trouble, so they had left the boat to try to get to civilization, and ultimately back to Florida as quickly as possible, where they were planning to deny any knowledge of the *Sylva*'s whereabouts. They had left the poor lady alone aboard the boat to fend for herself. As far as I was concerned that was the most miserable thing they had done. I was perfectly ready to pass over their maritime escapade, but the fact that they had abandoned their friend to her fate made them the blackest of criminals to me.

Florida is only seventy or eighty miles from Grand Bahama, and if the men had made it to Freeport and to the airport, they might well have gotten away with their mischief. Evidently they had not seemed at all contrite about taking the boat illegally or about leaving the lady. Nor had they been thankful for ending up aground in the safety of the Bahamas instead of what could have happened. They could have awakened to find themselves way out in the ocean, out of fuel, being thrown about by huge waves with no land in sight. They didn't appreciate how lucky they were to have ended up where they did.

The seaplane was now taking them to Nassau where they would be turned over to the American authorities and from where they would be flown back to Florida. The police had told Daddy that they would be charged with stealing the *Sylva*.

A week later the *Sylva*'s owner arrived at Deep Water Cay and thanked Daddy and the guides for helping to recover his boat. He gave money to everyone concerned, and on top of that he paid Daddy a week's dock rental for the *Sylva*. He then left with the *Sylva*, bound for Florida.

We never found out exactly what happened to the men and the lady, except of course that the crew man lost his job on the *Sylva*. I was certain the lady would have been so upset at the men for leaving her alone on the boat that she would have stopped being friends with both of them. I also thought she would have made a promise never to get drunk again, or at the very least, never to go out in a boat if she did get drunk again. The incident may have had a sad effect on her and the men's lives, but it made all of us feel like heroes. It was the favorite topic of conversation for a long time, and from then on, Kenneth walked with a new sense of pride in his step.

CHAPTER SIXTEEN

Ballet in the Basement

When it rained, we stayed indoors and read or played with the few toys and games we had. Some of the guests were extremely generous, and as a special way of saying thank you to my parents, they would send something for us children. One day three huge boxes arrived from Freeport, one for each of us. Inside Robin's was a furry golden lion, inside Joel's a huggable brown bear, and inside mine an elegant white poodle, larger than life. The people who sent them to us had been recent guests at Deep Water Cay. The man owned a huge company which manufactured soft toys. Besides the three large animals for us, he had included about a dozen smaller animals. We gave these to the kitchen ladies, to be distributed among their children. The animals really were lovely. My large fluffy poodle somehow made me feel linked to other children who I imagined had similar animals of their own.

I had a vivid imagination and the ability to play at make-believe for hours on end. I made princess dresses out of scraps of clothing and created my own secret gardens with a few flower blossoms and palm fronds. We did not have a television or a proper radio, so we had to invent most of our games. Daddy taught us how to play chess, and another nice guest gave us a Labyrinthspel, a clever wooden game that tested coordination skills to the limit. We all became whizzes at the game and impressed the guests who were new to it.

We played jacks, chess, checkers; we could hopscotch and hula-hoop; and of course, we played endless games on the sand and in the water. Robin and Joel and I talked about what we would be when we grew up. I knew very definitely that I was going to be an actress, an opera singer, a dancer, a poet, a writer, and an artist, and of course, I was going to get married and have children too. We would live in a huge house and have lots of friends who would come over, and we would perform impromptu plays and give impromptu concerts for each other. We would also have lots of pets, and I would invent clever gadgets.

During one of my daydreams, I hit upon the idea of creating a ballet for the guests. Sometimes I played my recorder for them in the evenings after they had come in from fishing, and I also read my poetry to them. They seemed to like being entertained, and so I thought, why not a ballet?

Obviously there was a limited cast, but fortunately there was a three-year-old girl staying on the island for an extended holiday. She was the niece of the owner and her name was Tracey. We all adored Tracey, who had a mop of blonde curls, bright blue eyes, and a lisp. I struck upon the perfect idea: We could portray the four seasons in dance while singing our own music.

We decided to use the basement, which was empty except for the ping-pong table and a dart board. The basement was not entirely underground; one side nestled into the slope of the garden while the other looked out over the mud flats. We stretched a string across the middle of the room and pinned some sheets onto it for the curtains.

With the help of Mommy and Robin and Joel, I set about devising the costumes and the action. Soon the costumes were assembled. Tracey was to wear my lace half-petticoat around her shoulders with a garland of flowers in her hair. She would be a daisy. I would wear a red full-circle skirt around my shoulders and a garland in my hair, and I would be a red rose.

Robin, who would be a butterfly, had the most gorgeous costume. While in Florida we had visited the Seminole tribe of Indians who lived in the Everglades. It was very special that we had been allowed to see them, because they did not encourage tourists--we had gone in with a missionary who knew the tribe. The Indians sewed the most amazing clothes, using strips of brightly colored fabric, making patterns of stylized waves, lightning, rain, sun, and so on. Mommy had bought Robin and me each a skirt and a bright jacket for Joel. Robin wore the jacket and a pair of tights, and pinned a skirt on either arm for large wings. She looked wonderful.

Joel was to be the weather. Spring would be rain falling on the flowers, and for spring rain, he would toss torn bits of tinfoil into the air. For summer he would be the sun and scatter sunbeams (cut up bits of yellow paper). Autumn would see the death of the daisy and the rose, plus all the leaves falling. (We collected what seemed like hundreds of the flat, fanlike sea grape leaves for Joel to toss into the air.) Winter would be frost and snow covering the poor dead bodies of the flowers. This time it was bits of white paper, and Joel was dressed like Jack Frost. He had to make whooshing noises like the north wind and swirl around spreading the snow.

We had several rehearsals, which I tended to direct. This was because I was bursting with ideas and knew exactly what I wanted. Robin and Joel were usually content for me to be the bossy one. The musical accompaniment would be each of us humming our own music. Mommy would act as curtain puller and prop lady.

We were excited about the ballet and could hardly wait for opening night. When all the props were ready, and we felt sure of what each of us was supposed to be doing, we announced the ballet to the guests. We called it "The Four Seasons," and everyone on the island was invited.

The ballet was so popular that we decided to do some drama as well. In November we performed a Guy Fawkes Night Special. One of the guests was involved and he acted as director and played Guy Fawkes; I was Robert Catesby, and Robin and Joel were various other characters.

We drew programs for the evening, and I wrote a Guy Fawkes poem:

> Guy Fawkes bent down his wicked head
> And for his life he did beg.
> But pity for he,
> He got none from we!
> Off came his arms,
> And then came his leg!

As Guy Fawkes and I crept toward the Palace of Westminster, I remember coming out with the line, "Let us act upon this act," which for some reason made the audience roar with laughter. Perhaps it was the absence of competition that made our shows so popular.

Next we presented a Christmas show. Mommy was the director, and Robin and Joel and I, quite originally, were the Three Wise Men. Heavily costumed and made-up, we formed an impressive procession while singing "We Three Kings of Orient Are." Tracey, once again with us, was the Christmas Angel.

Then came a highly successful, dramatized version of *The Cat in The Hat* by Dr. Seuss. Robin was the incredibly naughty and supercilious cat, getting Joel and me, as the two young children, into dreadful trouble, and out again--just in the nick of time before our mother came home. Robin wore a black leotard and tights, with an outsize and suitably floppy hat, a perky bow tie, and a long black tail which she wielded at times like a policeman's cudgel.

Those were our major performances for the guests, but amongst ourselves we were always dressing up and acting out wonderful fantasies. It was simply the best form of entertainment we had.

CHAPTER SEVENTEEN

Fools and Horses

By our second year on Deep Water Cay, I had exhausted nearly all the books for children, and I started reading the books that were kept for the guests. These were mainly detective stories by authors such as Ellery Queen, Agatha Christie, Ngaio Marsh, Ian Fleming, and many others. Without Mommy or Daddy really noticing, I picked them off the shelves and devoured them. Some of them scared me silly, and I would go around for days glancing behind my back or creeping timidly into dark rooms, almost too frightened to turn on the light.

One of the books on the shelves was the complete works of Edgar Allan Poe. I read it from cover to cover. For quite a while after that my poetry sounded oddly reminiscent of Poe. I wrote lugubrious ballads about dying maidens, and depressive love poems. Happily that stage did not last very long. Some of the paperbacks were about espionage, and I began to toy with the idea that I should become a spy. I liked the idea of disguising myself and carrying out all sorts of dangerous and important missions. I experimented with accents and I practiced walking without a sound. Therefore, it was quite natural that I decided to do some special dressing up for April Fool's Day.

I lighted upon the idea to try to fool Daddy. I would disguise myself as a tourist from Freeport, a lone middle-aged lady out for a day's jaunt. I decided she should be rather over made-up, which would assist with my disguise, and well stacked, which would also help with the deception. I was just ten years old and still as flat as a pancake. In fact most of the time I ran around in just a pair of shorts. Puberty was a year away, and I exulted in my freedom, little realizing how soon it was to end. Mommy had already started to tell me to put on a shirt when guests were on the island.

I needed Mommy's help with my idea to fool Daddy, and she became my chief ally. The first task was to change my hair. I would have to do more than tie a scarf around my head to fool my own father. Together Mommy and I thought hard and struck upon the idea of using Evalina's wig. Evalina usually wore a wig on the island because she had very short hair, too short even to plait. She willingly agreed to let me borrow her precious wig. It was jet black with tight curls and smelt of the kitchen, but it was perfect.

Next, the clothing. This was slightly more difficult. Daddy

would have seen all my clothes and all of Mommy's or Robin's. But Mommy came up with a brilliant idea. She took a short-sleeved jacket of hers and turned it inside out. The lining was bright orange terry-cloth, and we were sure Daddy would not recognize it. We discovered one of Mommy's blouses, rarely worn and fairly nondescript, which would do for underneath the jacket. The most fun was designing the bosoms. Mommy adjusted one of her bras to fit around me, and we stuffed the cups with scrunched up socks. The effect was staggering, and we hoped that it would inspire Daddy's gaze not to linger on my face, which we knew would be the most difficult to disguise.

But disguise it we did! Because the wig was dark and I was tanned, we used a heavy hand with the cosmetics. Mommy furnished some glaring red lipstick and dug up some blue and black make-up for my eyes. I was unrecognizable. I felt that I looked like a clown, but Mommy was sure I could pass for a certain type of woman. We completed the outfit with some anonymous beige trousers, and I wore a pair of Mommy's sandals, hoping that Daddy would not even see my feet. I decided on a soft, breathy way of speaking, with a whiff of foreign accent. "Foreign" meant an indeterminate East-European accent.

We planned the trick in great detail. On April Fool's Day right before lunch, Mommy would find Daddy, who was usually in the lodge at that time. It was important that he be kept up at the lodge; otherwise he would know if a boat had been asked to ferry anyone over from the mainland. I would slip into the bar and up onto one of the bar stools. Mommy would tell Daddy that a day guest had arrived from Freeport and had asked for a dry martini. Daddy was very good at making dry martinis. Our goal was to get Daddy actually to make the drink. If we succeeded in that, we would consider that the deception had worked.

The day came and I got dressed. Mommy made up my face, and we positioned the wig. I slipped out of the front of the lodge and ran down a back way to the dock, so I could turn around and stroll leisurely back to the lodge on the proper paved pathway which all the guests used. I arrived at the main entrance again where Mommy was waiting for me. We could not be sure if Daddy might suddenly appear from the back room, so Mommy spoke to me as if I were a guest. As she led me into the bar, she asked how I had enjoyed the trip over and where I lived. I answered her sweetly in my foreign voice. To anyone passing by, it would have seemed like a perfectly genuine conversation. There was only one small problem. Mommy had great difficulty stifling a giggle whenever she saw me, and she had to struggle to control the corners of her mouth. But she got me into the bar, straightened her face, and went off to fetch Daddy.

I was perching on one of the bar stools and gazing out the window when Daddy walked in. He entered the bar through the door leading in from the kitchen. "How do, how do," he said, by way of a greeting. I turned my head to him and tilted it charmingly. I was a woman of few words. I sat very straight, my chest protruding over the bar, my bright red lips pouting coquettishly. Daddy had started to prepare the dry martini. "Are you over for long?" he asked. "Oh no," I said, with my faint whiff of indeterminate East-European accent, "just for the day."

I was giving nothing away, and my poor father had to struggle with the conversation. He tried again. "Did you want to go bonefishing?" I gave him a sweet dismissive smile and said, "Oh no, I just want to walk on your beautiful island."

Suddenly from behind us there came a strange sound, like someone being smothered or strangled. I ignored the sound and turned to stare dreamily out the window. But Daddy's head shot up to discover Mommy peeking around the doorway, unable to stay away. The sight of her husband mixing a drink for her ten-year-old daughter was too much for her. Mommy had started to giggle. Daddy glared at her over my head, wriggling his eyebrows as much as he dared to signal her to stop. Mommy disappeared around the corner. Daddy adjusted his expression and went back to putting the finishing touches on the drink. "Do you come from Freeport?" he asked politely. "Yes," I answered, "I come from Freeport. I live there now."

Our conversation was interrupted by another explosion of giggles from Mommy, who was once again peeking around the doorway. Daddy glanced at her and then glanced back at me to see if I was aware of this rude eavesdropper. Then I made a mistake. I turned around briefly to look at Mommy. There she was, propped up against the side of the doorway, shaking with silent laughter, tears running down her face. Daddy was making a fearsome face at her, as if to say, "Go away--even if she looks appalling, she's still a guest. Don't let her see you laughing at her!"

It was too much for me. I choked down a giggle. Daddy turned from Mommy to me, confused. Then he froze and stared at me, recognition slowly dawning. His face went bright pink, and he put down the drink that he was just about to hand me. Then he said, "Oh my gosh" in a shocked and stunned sort of voice and walked out of the bar by the bartender's door.

Mommy and I collapsed in shrieks of laughter. I nearly fell off the stool and staggered to Mommy, both of us holding our sides and hooting with laughter. A second later Daddy emerged from the kitchen. He had the most sheepish, lopsided grin on his face I had ever seen. "April Fool," I gasped, "April Fool!" Daddy came closer to inspect me, his eyes registering total incredulity.

Mommy was still bent double and sobbing with mirth. Daddy went pinker and pinker, until he too burst out laughing. Robin and Joel and the ladies in the kitchen came in to view the spectacle. They stood around me laughing and laughing while Mommy, constantly interrupting herself with fresh shrieks of laughter, tried to explain how Daddy had fallen for the bait. No one could believe that I had really fooled my own father. It was quite a coup, the best stunt I had ever done.

Years later, when I was about fifteen, I tried the trick again, only slightly altered. Dressed as an older woman, I banged on the door of our house and sobbed that I had just crashed my car and could I please telephone my husband. Daddy again fell for it, and immediately called for Mommy to come and minister to me. The following year I fooled him as well as some neighbors and one of my teachers with a similar prank.

Needless to say, that first April Fool's joke became famous at Deep Water Cay, and the story was told and retold many, many times. Photographs were taken of me in my garb, and even though I look quite alarming, I still cannot see how I was able to fool my own father!

As it turned out, I was not the only one to pull off successful deceptive stunts. Robin and one of her friends were the stars of another incident. This is really Robin's story, but she told it to me so many times that I can imagine every minute of it.

While living at Deep Water Cay, we learned about some of the many local superstitions. One of the most powerful legends was that of the White Horse. For as long as anyone could remember, there had always been the White Horse. Supposedly, from time to time an evil ghost horse and rider would gallop through the tiny villages and terrorize everyone. The villagers would close their shutters in the evenings so the White Horse would not get them. I do not think that anyone had ever been gotten, at least within living memory, but no one took any chances with the dreaded White Horse.

Our family had become very good friends with a French-Canadian family, the Cartiers, who lived about fifty miles away from us on the southeastern tip of Grand Bahama. Every so often we would make the journey to visit them, a journey which involved crossing over from Deep Water Cay by boat, and then bumping down the fifty miles in an old van on a dirt road that was pitted with the most enormous potholes. The Cartiers had a daughter, Joan, about Robin's age. Robin and Joan became firm friends. I always felt left out around them. There was no room in their friendship for kid sisters.

One week Robin was invited to stay with the Cartiers. She was about twelve at the time. I think Joan had already turned thirteen, which made her seem unreachable, a breed apart. It was the last week of October and Robin was to stay over Halloween.

On Halloween night Robin and Joan decided to dress up and have some fun. They hit upon the idea of dressing up as ghosts and dressing Joan's donkey as a ghost and riding through the nearest village as the White Horse. Joan spirited some old sheets from her mother's linen cupboard, and she and Robin prepared for the night. They cut eyeholes for themselves in two of the sheets and larger eyeholes in a sheet for the donkey.

After supper, Joan, Robin, and the donkey crept out of the garden and started down the dirt road to the village. It was dusk and the sun had sunk beneath the horizon. The light was fading fast, leaving a pink and mauve glow in the sky. The hot land was cooling and a mist was rising. It was perfect weather for spooks!

By the time the eerie threesome had drawn close to the village, all the color had faded from the bushes and trees, and the country was just dark shape upon dark shape, against an inky purple sky. Everything was quiet except for the sound of the donkey's hooves on the dirt road, the chirping and humming of the insects, and the occasional call of a night heron in the nearby swamp. The girls prepared for their raid. Joan mounted her white-clad beast, and Robin stood poised alongside. They were off!

With wild whoops and evil-sounding screeches, they galloped through the row of houses, sheets billowing and hooves pounding. The reaction they received was evidently most gratifying. Doors slammed, and screams could be heard from within the houses. Babies awoke and wailed. Dogs went into barking frenzies. The village was in panic.

Once through the village and out of sight, Joan slowed the donkey to a walk and Robin stopped running. They were panting and laughing in victory. They had succeeded in tricking the village into thinking the White Horse had paid a visit. It was no small feat for two young girls, and they were elated with the success of their mischief.

After waiting for the chaos in the village to die down, Robin and Joan turned back for home, this time without the sheets. I don't believe they even got into trouble, despite disappearing without permission and taking the donkey and cutting holes into three sheets. Perhaps the Cartiers were impressed by their pluck.

News soon reached Deep Water Cay that the White Horse had ridden out on All Saints' Eve but mercifully had not grabbed anyone. We heard how the terrifying specter had thundered through the village, shrieking evil obscenities while it tried to kidnap a villager. The stories grew and grew and revived the fears and superstitions of all the people in the area. It was really rather wicked of the girls, but even my parents could not find it in themselves to be cross.

I always felt a glow of pride for Robin when we heard the legend being talked about, but not one of us ever let on what we knew about the most recent ride of the White Horse.

CHAPTER EIGHTEEN

Going to Church

Besides being extremely superstitious, the Bahamians tended to be very religious. They had no doubts as to who it was that kept them alive through hurricanes, diseases, and accidents. And if the storms or diseases or accidents claimed lives, they knew to whom they could turn.

God was real to the villagers of MacLeans Town in a special way. They could see God when their crops grew. They knew God to be with them when they had to make crossings in rough seas. God was in their families, in the love and joy they shared. And God always had open ears and a big heart and would listen to their prayers with a great tenderness. Above everything, God knew. God knew when they were hurting and suffering. God knew when things were especially tough for them. And the deep ocean of His understanding and compassion would see them through the bad times. The people of MacLeans Town did not only go to God when they were in trouble. They ran to Him in joy during the good times as well.

To a large extent their view of God was also my view of God. I thanked God in private when things went well. I pleaded with Him to spare our lives during the fierce thunderstorms which rolled over our island many hot afternoons. I begged Him to spare our lives when we went skin diving or sailing in rough seas. I secretly thanked Him when I wrote a good poem, or when Mommy and Daddy chose to make peace instead of war.

God was in the brilliant purple and orange sunsets which lit up the evening skies. He made the shells, my favorite sculptures of nature. He made the bright fish and the sea fans and the warm sea. It was clear to me that God had made everything and that He took great delight in His creation. I could not understand when nature went against me, when there were the violent storms, when mosquitoes bit, when fish were poisonous, when Mouser went mad, when Ladybug died. Why, God. . .? Mommy tried to explain.

It was something about God not interfering with the world as it was, and something dark and disturbing about people having ruined things long ago. I fantasized a world where snakes did not bite, where sharks were friendly, where the sun never burned, and there was no death and dying. I longed for my paradise where there would be no stings and barbs and sharp teeth. I knew Jesus was very important and that He held the key. I loved Him and His Father passionately, almost the way I loved my parents. Somehow, I knew I never had to really worry, worry unto death, if my parents and God were around. I could frolic in the water, skip across the land, and sink exhausted into my bed at night, secure in the knowledge that God was in control.

We said grace at every meal, and we took turns saying it. My mother's sister, our Aunt Jan, had sent us a small wooden box filled with tiny paper scolls. Each scroll was printed with a verse from the Bible, a promise of something good. The box had written on the top in gold letters, "Precious Promises." I loved that box, as we all did, and we memorized our favorite promises until the little scrolls were tattered, and we could recognize them just by the way they were worn.

We said family prayers together every night, usually gathered on Mommy and Daddy's bunks, curled up to them for the last burst of affection for the night. The prayer time began with each of us saying our own spontaneous prayers, followed by the Lord's Prayer. Then we took turns choosing a hymn to sing. We sang without books or music. Mommy had taught us many of the standard Anglican hymns as we had sailed. Then we all kissed one another and went to our individual bunks.

While on the boat, we would ask Mommy or Daddy (though it was usually Mommy) question after question about what God was like, why the world was the way it was, and what pleased God. We learned about the characters from the Old Testament: Moses, Noah, Abraham, Jacob, Rachel, Ruth, Esther. We heard the stories from the New Testament, all about Jesus and His friends and enemies. I thought of Jesus as someone who did not speak very often but who, if turned to, would always be there and always have the right answer.

I imagined His eyes, and I imagined that they would be full of love. Jesus would never send me away and never ignore me. I knew that I could make Him and His Father, God, very happy by being good and cheerful and helpful and kind and generous. They would also be happy when I forgot about everything and just played or swam without worry, happily lost in Their creation. And I knew that when I was bad, I hurt God, and Jesus would turn to me with His loving eyes and say nothing, just look at me with deep disappointment. I wanted to make God happy, I wanted to make Him laugh, I wanted Him to be glad He had made me.

Since there was no church on Deep Water Cay, we had to travel to the small church in MacLeans Town. We could not go every Sunday, sometimes because of the guests, and sometimes because the water was too rough to make the crossing. Going to church was a big production, and I half loved it and half dreaded it.

We had to get up early in the morning and put on our best clothes. Robin and I would take out our dresses and slip them over our heads, enjoying the strangeness of it. Dresses and socks and shoes were very special. When we were ready and had eaten a hurried breakfast of cereal or scrambled eggs on toast, we would run down to the dock and climb into one of the outboard motorboats. We had to take wet-weather gear, just in case. Mommy usually took a Bible.

After pounding across the waves for nearly half an hour, we would arrive at MacLeans Town, where there would always be someone to take our rope and tie us to the old dock. Our presence created a stir whenever we went to church. We were the only white people within miles, and certainly the only white people who ever came to that church. We children would walk shyly behind our parents, who would be chatting to the welcoming committee. The doors of the small white-washed building were always left open, and dogs and chickens came in and out all through the services. Nearly everyone in the entire village went to church: babies, young children, older children, grownups, and very old people, some who could not see very well and had to walk with old sticks for canes. It was impossible for us to take our seats quietly and unobserved, even if we were late and the service had already started. The moment we came in, all eyes would turn to us, and many of them would stay riveted on us during the entire service.

Then came the most embarrassing bit. After a hymn or before the next reading, the preacher would suddenly announce, beaming broadly, "Brothers and sisters, we have with us this morning Brother and Sister Muller and their fine young children." (Intense embarrassment would be experienced by us children.) "Brother and Sister Muller, would you have a few words for us this morning?" His words would be punctuated and nearly drowned by the steady chorus of "Amens" which the adults kept up throughout the service. First Daddy would stand up, clear his throat, (this was not his favorite part either), and say a bit about how privileged we were to be able to come and worship with them. Then Mommy would rise nervously, (Mommy treated these occasions like performances and always got nervous), and say how much we loved to worship with them. Depending on how family life had been, she would either give a nice, short, and gracious thank you, or she would be overcome by all the love and emotion and choke up with tears.

There was something profoundly moving about seeing a

church full of people dressed in ragged clothes and worn-out shoes looking up at us with radiant faces, wanting nothing from us, but giving us love and acceptance in abundance. Even I could feel it. It was completely devastating, and Mommy would end up dabbing at her eyes with her handkerchief more often than not. Even though we were accepted as fellow Christians, equal before God, we were treated like special guests.

Once the embarrassing welcome and mandatory speeches were over, I could relax into the service. The preacher always went on too long for me, and I got lost in the many spontaneous prayers, but there was an excitement about the service. Going to church was the one time a week when the people could rest from their unrewarding, and for many of them, backbreaking, work, and release all their feelings. Women wept and moaned, and men sobbed in their pews, their large gnarled hands wiping away the tears. Old women would rock back and forth and wail. Babies would whimper and cry, and the chickens screech. Sometimes, when a woman would sob particularly loudly, the vicar and some other men and women would go to her and hold her and pray loudly for her until the sobbing subsided. It was a strange but somehow orderly bedlam, each person being purged from the burdens and sorrows and pain of the past week, each letting the others do likewise.

Robin and Joel and I were bug-eyed throughout these services. It was like taking part in a group therapy session, mixed with prayers, Bible readings, a sermon, and singing. The few hymn books they had were old and falling apart. There were only a few Bibles in the entire village, and the people who owned them were considered to be extra blessed.

My favorite parts of the services were the hymns. A man or a woman would burst into song, unannounced, and soon other voices would take it up, swelling to a rich organ-like sound trembling in my ears. It was beautiful singing, straight from the heart and utterly sincere. They sang what they felt--and they danced. People would sway in time with the music and start a soft shuffle on the bare earth floor. Sometimes there would be clapping as well, and then the sound would flood out of the church and over the water. On the Sundays that we did not go to church, sometimes we would listen for the singing. If the wind was in the right direction and not too fierce, we could hear the singing coming to us over the water, a song floating like a spirit.

When we sang, I would try to sing just like the Bahamians, broad and rich and mellow. I would stand and sway and let the music drench me with its tangible presence. My favorite hymn was one called "We Are Out on the Ocean Sailing." It made me cry, even then.

We are out on the ocean sailing,
Homeward bound we swiftly glide.
We are out on the ocean sailing
To a home beyond the tide.

All the storms will soon be over,
Then we'll anchor in the harbour.
We are out on the ocean sailing,
To a home beyond the tide.

I felt as if that was just what we were doing, literally and figuratively, sailing on an ocean, with heaven as the harbor we would all get to some day. Whatever my fears and hurts, singing that song would acknowledge them and then take them all away, far out to sea, and leave them there for the winds to blow away.

Departing from church at the end of a service involved another ritual. The services would sometimes last up to three hours. It took a long time for the village to be put right for another week. At the end of these marathons, the villagers would swarm around us, stroking our hair and touching our cheeks. Then we would all squeeze out of the church, and an impromptu receiving line would form around the doors. We were expected to go down the line, each of us shaking hands with everyone.

It was not a matter of a simple short handshake; rather, it was a short dance while holding hands. The people would stand waiting for us, hopping and swaying from foot to foot according to their inner rhythms. Some people jiggled quickly and bounced energetically from foot to foot. Others swayed slowly and swung our hands in theirs in a graceful dance. The trick was to try to match each person's rhythm. Saying good-bye like this seemed a way for each person to share with us something of him or herself. If we could clasp hands and shake them, somehow we had met on a deeper plane. However, some of the churchgoers were even more shy of us than we were of them. When it came time to shake their hands, it was a case of brushing our palms together lightly, eyes lowered.

There was another thing that interested me about going to church. When we children outgrew our clothes, Mommy gave them to the ladies in the kitchen to be dispensed in town. It was a rather good game to look around in church and see who was wearing my clothes. The people of MacLeans Town had so little, and every new gift stuck out like a sore thumb, until it too wore out or faded in the sun.

My parents were touched by the Bahamians' love of their Bibles and the obvious need for more Bibles and more prayer books. They wrote to a church back in America asking them to send Bibles. After a few months, a boxful of secondhand Bibles arrived. My parents took them over to MacLeans Town and passed them out with the help of the vicar. It was as if the people had received a gift straight from heaven. They were desperately proud of their new books, and so thankful. They loved Mommy and Daddy anyway, but this served to increase the love and deepen the bonds of affection. After that Mommy and Daddy asked for more Bibles to be sent, and whenever we sailed to a new island, we would give them away. The looks on the people's faces told me that these books were more precious to them than almost anything else in the world. Some people hugged them and wept. For some, it was the first time they had ever held a Bible, much less owned one.

We would come back from our churchgoing full of hymns and friendly faces, but also tired and drained and glad to be back among familiar surroundings with our own familiar habits. I rarely go to churches now like the one at MacLeans Town, but when I do, I am aware of the sense of having come home.

CHAPTER NINETEEN

Rickie

Because Robin and Joel and I usually had only each other, we missed out on the jokes, tales, and general chatter about boy and girl stuff and all that. But even left to our own devices, we found enough to keep us occupied. For a while another boat was moored at the dock on Deep Water Cay. A man and woman lived aboard. Exactly what they were doing on the island and why they stayed so long I have no idea, but unwittingly the lady provided us with some clandestine entertainment.

One night at dusk, as we were fishing late on the dock, we glanced into the portholes of the boat which was lit from within. There, to our extreme delight, we could see the lady undressing. She peeled off her blouse and stripped off her shorts and there she was, stark naked. She must have been too warm, because she went about the business of fixing their dinner in the nude as if nothing was out of the ordinary. We three were used to seeing Mommy in this state, but when Mommy got too warm, at least she used to leave on her underpants. To see another woman with nothing on was somehow terribly exotic and exciting. We crouched motionless on the dock, staring and gawking through the tiny round portholes at the woman oblivious to her rapt audience.

When it got too dark, we had to go up to the lodge where we knew Mommy and Daddy would be expecting us. Of course, we said nothing to them; this was our secret. After that, when we could, we would slip down to the dock at dusk in the hopes of seeing the same sight through the portholes, and on several nights we were not disappointed. It made me blink a bit, seeing the lady afterwards up on deck in the daylight, properly clothed, because I knew what was underneath. We considered it good fun while it lasted, but one day the couple sailed their boat off into the distance, and that was the last we saw of them.

At about this time, I decided I would like to have a bikini. Usually I swam in panties or one-piece bathing suits, but I felt the time had come for a more sophisticated swimsuit. Of course there were no shops, so I knew I would have to make it myself. I asked if I could have some material from Mommy's sewing bag, and I rummaged until I found a few pieces of sage green corduroy, large enough for the intended article. I fashioned two triangles for the top, and a large double triangle joined at one of the corners for the bottoms. The only problem was how to fasten it. With a flash of inspiration, I ran to the ribbon box where I kept all my hair bands and ribbons and chose ten ribbons, all of different colors. With two I made the shoulder straps, with two more I made the back straps, and with another two I connected the pieces of the bra. With the remaining four I fastened the ties for my hips. It was finished.

I tried it on in secret in our bathroom, admiring my handiwork in the mirror. I loved it and I felt infinitely more grown up than I did in my old one-piece, even though my one-piece at that time was in a very chic leopard-skin pattern. Proudly, with head held high, I went to show off my creation to Mommy and to anyone else who would look at it.

Mommy was decidedly lukewarm about my bikini. While praising me for my ingenuity, she definitely did not put her stamp of approval on the garment as a whole. She thought I was much too young to be wearing a bikini, and anyway she disliked bikinis on anyone. She used to mutter about how they cut the hips right at the most unattractive line and about how most women looked silly in them. But even at that age I could detect a whiff of censoriousness in her views. I could tell that she did not like bikinis because they showed off too much body.

Feeling somewhat deflated, I took myself and my bikini down to the beach for an inaugural dip. It felt exciting swimming in the bikini, feeling the water on my belly in a new way. I splashed around happily for a while before I decided it was time for lunch, or if not lunch, then at least a snack. To my great horror, when I stood up, my bikini sagged terribly with the weight of the water and revealed all the bits of me which it had been specifically designed to cover up. I clutched at the waterlogged bottoms and hoisted them up in what I knew was not a very sophisticated manner, rearranging the limp triangles of the top so they would see me safely and modestly into the lodge.

I scampered back to our rooms, leaving a trail of wet footprints and little trickles of water across the living room floor. The corduroy had not been a good choice of material for my bikini. It dawned on me that I had never seen another bathing suit in corduroy and that perhaps I had discovered the reason why. I accepted defeat. I had created a beautiful but totally useless garment. If only Mommy had some scraps of a nice, lightweight, stretchy fabric, but she did not.

That was it for my bikini-making, and I went back resignedly to my leopard-skin one-piece, still longing for a garment which would help make me feel as grown-up on the outside as I was beginning to feel on the inside.

Not long after that, someone definitely helped me begin to feel very special and much more grown up. From time to time a family called Hayward came to Deep Water Cay. They divided their time between England and a huge gorgeous home in Freeport. We had met and become friends when we lived in Freeport, and they came to visit us several times while we lived on Deep Water Cay.

The Haywards had a son, Rickie, and he and I had become firm friends during our brief encounters. Rickie was about two years older than I, which, of course, made him seem somewhat mysterious to me. He was tall and slender, with dark brown hair and bright blue eyes. When his family came to our island, his parents would take a walk or relax with a drink in the bar. That left Rickie and any other siblings or friends he may have brought with him to Robin and Joel and me.

Rickie and I always fell back into our friendship quite naturally. I remember taking him swimming off the beach near the dock. We laughed and played tag and dived for shells off the dock. We would chase each other down the beach and then fall laughing into the water. I was ten at the time, and playing with Rickie like this seemed to me a most agreeable way to spend a day. It was definitely more exciting than playing with my brother or sister. There was something special about this boy who could make me laugh. I made him laugh too as we twisted and turned in the water, spouting like whales, trying to catch each other's slippery bodies.

We had a contest to see who of us could hold our breath longer. I have no idea who won, but we both kept on giggling and spoiling our chances for breaking any records. Then we decided to swim under water with our eyes open and see if we could communicate with each other. Time and time again we would take a huge gulp of air and plunge beneath the surface to look at one another. We looked funny underwater trying to hold our breaths. Our hair floated upwards like seaweed, and our faces were contorted with trying to hold onto the air. Rickie and I would dive deep and then look at each other and giggle and have to come to the surface again.

On one of these visits, Rickie asked me, "Have you ever kissed anyone under water?" "No," I said. I had not really had the chance. "Come on," Rickie urged, and he put his arms around me. "Hold on to me, and let's try it." It sounded wonderful, so I wrapped my arms around his neck and my legs around his waist, and I took a big breath. Together we sank to the bottom, and there, about six feet under, we kissed each other. Then we started to rise to the surface, still holding on to each other. In a mass of bubbles and splashing, we came shooting up out of the water, laughing and gasping for breath. This was a jolly good game, and we plunged under the water again and again, two slippery water babies, arms and legs entwined, kissing each other and reveling in the sheer delight of it all.

Too soon someone came and called for Rickie. It was time for his family to leave. Our eyes were shining when we waved goodbye to each other, and there were promises to write.

For a while we wrote to each other. Then he went back to school in England, and he seemed so far away. I never saw him again, because we left Deep Water Cay before he returned. But Rickie had done something special for me. He had helped me take the first few steps on the rather shaky bridge that leads from childhood to adolescence, and he had made those steps joyous.

Suitable suitors were so few and far between that I can remember the only other likely candidate I met at Deep Water Cay. He was a bit older and came from America with his family, the Klopmans. I had heard of the Klopmans because they owned a large fabric and clothing enterprise in the States. The advertisements that appeared in magazines took up an entire page and showed the model leaning back on thin air and smiling confidently. The accompanying words said, "You can lean on a Klopman." I had always wondered how they took the photograph.

Peter Klopman was rather shy and quiet, and I felt instinctively that he liked me. Even though he was sixteen at the time, I sensed it was I who would have to help him become my friend. We went for walks, we swam (with no kisses), and we had halting conversations. Peter sought me out when the other members of his family were elsewhere, and he seemed to be pleading with me to know what to say or do. But I was too young and inexperienced and was even more hesitant than he. He wasn't like Rickie, who knew exactly what to do. There was a strange tortured feeling between us whenever we were together, a feeling I had never felt before. It made both of us intensely self-conscious and tongue-tied, even though it was certainly fascinating and oddly pleasurable.

The Klopman parents got along particularly well with Mommy and Daddy, and before they left, Mommy took some photographs of our families together. In one, Peter stands not far from me, his head inclined toward me, as if indicating with whom his interest lay.

After about a month or two, a box came for us. It contained a beautiful blouse each for Mommy and Robin and me. My blouse was pale pink and made of a light chiffon, with buttons up the back. It made me feel elegant and grown-up.

I decided if Peter ever came back, I would suggest we kiss each other, as that was the only thing I knew to do. But he never came again, and I finished my days on Deep Water Cay a solitary mermaid, diving and dancing with only the fish for my friends.

CHAPTER TWENTY

Christmas in Florida

Guests came and went from our tiny paradise, and with the exception of Rickie, they barely interrupted my concentration on shells, books, plays, and the many other activities with which I busied myself. But one of the guests made a big impact on my life, a girl named Deborah Kane, who came to visit with her parents. Deborah was a girl of just my age, which at that time was nearly ten. I don't remember her having any brothers or sisters. She was an American from Florida. She had lovely, shiny, wavy, light-brown hair and a lightly freckled, smiling face. Her eyes were large and bright blue, and she had a small, neatly formed nose and a mouth like a little strawberry. I thought she was wonderful, and we became firm friends at once, spending every waking hour together while her parents were out fishing or being sociable in the bar with the other guests.

I took Deborah swimming and shelling on the beach. At first she was a little timid, but soon she was splashing about quite happily, even though she tired of playing in the water sooner than I the water sooner than I did. But then I was half fish anyway. I showed her all my treasures, and talked with her about everything on my mind. I liked talking about clothes and making things and planning adventures. We both had Barbie dolls, and we dressed our Barbies and constructed situations for them and dreamed of how we would look when we grew up.

When it was time for the Kanes to fly back to Florida, I was sad at the thought of saying good-bye to Deborah, but she seemed even more devastated and kept on talking about how she wished I could come and visit her. "That would be wonderful," I said, not thinking about it as a real possibility. After all, Deborah lived in Florida and I lived on Deep Water Cay, and that was that. If we wanted to see each other, we had to wait until her parents came fishing again. I was quite at peace with the facts. Perhaps I had had more experience at saying goodbye to friends and moving on from person to person, since I had moved on so often from port to port.

A few weeks after the Kanes had gone home, my mother received a letter from Mrs. Kane. She read it with excitement spreading across her face. "Christina," she exclaimed, "the Kanes have invited you to spend Christmas with them in Florida." What a fabulous invitation!--a trip just for me! It made me feel so grown-up just to be asked. Mommy and Daddy were excited for me too and said they thought that it was a splendid idea. Robin and Joel were amazed and thought I was very lucky. It did not take long for me to make up my mind, and Mommy wrote back saying I would love to come.

The Kanes must have been very rich, but I did not notice wealth then. They arranged for me to be collected from Deep Water Cay by an amphibian plane and then flown across the Gulf Stream to Florida, where they would pick me up at an airport near their home.

Mommy helped me plan my wardrobe, and for the first time in a long time, I had to think about clean socks and good shoes, pretty dresses and a purse, and other things I rarely needed in Deep Water Cay. Mommy kept on reminding me about good manners, as if she had never told me before, and about being helpful to Mrs. Kane, and about being generally neat and tidy in someone else's home. Of course, I had heard all these things umpteen times before, and I knew them by heart, but I listened anyway, just excited at the prospect of being in Florida with Deborah.

At last, about a week before Christmas, the big day arrived. It had come much more quickly than I expected, and up until the actual morning, the whole trip had not seemed entirely real to me. It was more like an elaborate game I had been playing, just imagining getting ready and packing my suitcase. In a way, it felt almost too normal to be real. Certainly on the morning I was going to fly by myself across miles of ocean to visit a faraway friend, I should have felt transformed, somehow like a different person. I certainly felt very excited, but I still felt just like me.

I got dressed in my best dress, one with dark navy and olive green stripes and some white lace trim, and Mommy brushed my hair and put it up in a topknot and tied a big red ribbon around it. I was to take a soft red leather drawstring bag covered in tiny gold stars. I had only a small suitcase. Florida was practically the same temperature as the Bahamas, so I did not have to pack any heavy sweaters or coats.

I ate breakfast with my stomach churning and my thoughts racing ahead. What would it be like to fly in the seaplane? Would I be frightened all by myself? What would it be like in Florida? What was Deborah's house like? And on and on . . . .

By late morning we could hear the sound of a faraway engine which grew louder and louder. I dashed out of the lodge and spotted the plane coming in low for a landing on the strip of water between the docks on Deep Water Cay and the mainland. It was a small silvery plane with some stripes on the sides, and it looked like a fat bird making a shallow dive into the water. It touched the water on its rounded belly and slowed down gently with waves spraying out from its bow. Gradually it turned and pointed its nose toward the small concrete landing strip on the beach, which was wide enough for boats or planes. The plane seemed to rise up out of the water as if by magic. But as it came up onto the landing strip, I could see it was driving up on wheels which extended down from the bottom of the plane. At last it was out of the water; dripping wet, it came to a slightly jerky stop at the top of the strip. It was an extraordinary machine: first a plane, then a boat, and now a car. I couldn't believe I was lucky enough to be going on a trip in that plane, and, what was more, it had come to Deep Water Cay just to pick me up. I was almost dizzy with the magnitude of the event.

The pilot emerged from the plane and beamed at the small crowd gathered round. He chatted with Daddy for awhile and then disappeared toward the lodge for a short time. I stayed by the plane, staring up at it and talking to Mommy and Robin and Joel and some of the guides and cooks who had come to be part of the farewell committee.

I felt a bit self-conscious, as so much of the activity was all for my benefit. It was a little like being in one of our home-produced skits. There were lines to be said, action that had to happen, and the drama had to proceed in a set way. The scene today was "Christina gets on a plane and flies off to Florida," and everyone was playing his or her part beautifully. There were goodbyes to be said, and many hugs and kisses with Mommy and Daddy, and even a few slightly embarrassed hugs with Robin and Joel. Even though we loved each other deeply, the three of us did not make a habit of going around hugging and kissing each other. But this was a special occasion and it deserved special treatment. Levi, one of the guides, was as proud of me as if I were his own daughter.

When all was ready, the pilot announced it was time to go. I stood on one of the steps leading up to the plane and turned and waved at my family. Levi stood beside me, ushering me in as if I were a fairytale princess stepping into a fairytale coach. I gave a grand last wave from the top of the steps and stepped eagerly into the small plane. Already it was as if I had entered a new world, and even though there were only the thin metal sides of the plane separating me from the outside world, it felt to me as if I had entered a time warp, almost as if everyone on the outside had ceased to exist, or as if they were in a different dimension. Inside I found several seats, but the pilot suggested I sit with him. He and I were the only people in the plane. He showed me how to strap myself in and then he started the engine and we began to ease back into the water. I was almost deafened by the sound of the engines roaring in my ears. It was like being on a small enclosed motor boat, and we motored out from the beach until we were in the center of the inlet. I was torn between waving to my family, who were all waving madly to me, and concentrating on every move the pilot made.

Finally the pilot pointed the plane out to sea, and gradually we started to gain speed. I turned and waved to the small band of people who were still waving to me, the people I loved the most in the whole world, and I felt a strange flicker of something desperate in my heart. The ride was getting bumpier and bumpier, and the spray was splashing up onto the windows. I turned away from the group on the beach, and the pilot started to tell me what we were going to do next. I listened to his words in his calm, friendly voice and stared ahead, until all of a sudden, the pounding, speeding boat became a plane.

We rose out of the water and gained height so slowly that I thought we would never make it. The movement of the waves ceased, and we began to climb away from the water, rising higher and higher until we became the plane we were supposed to be. I looked back and down on Deep Water Cay and could see the tiny dots that were my family still waving. Instinctively I waved back, although I knew they could no longer see me. I noticed how different the shoreline looked from the air and how small it all seemed. Even the tall, bushy Australian pine tree, which usually towered over me when I played in the sand beneath its branches, seemed like a small garden bush, nothing special. The waves rolling up onto the beach made tiny creases of white appear, and then they too vanished. My world was spinning away from me in a haze of engine roar, and then it shrank slowly into just a solid line on the horizon behind us. I stopped looking back.

The flight was exhilarating. We flew over the deep pale green of the sand flats, the color of old turquoise which grew deeper and turned to aquamarine blue, then a deeper navy, and then, into the glowing mysterious impenetrable violet of deep water. When we sailed, it was a color that always excited me, because it signified we were away from the land, away from what we knew. It always scared me in a strange way, because it meant we were out over the unknown, out over the big fish, the sharks, and all the dwellers of the deep, and anything could happen. But in the plane, it felt very different from the crossing we had made on the *Tappan Zee* a few years earlier. The plane's engine made a loud steady buzzing, and I was lost in the wonder of flying, lost in the excitement of this adventure which I was going on all by myself.

After what seemed like only an hour or so, we spotted the coastline of Florida. My old country. I was suddenly filled with the desire to get there and see everything again. I forgot the mesmerizing effects of flying and of staring at the water beneath us. Now all I wanted to do was land and see Deborah. The pilot flew us to a small airport on land and brought us down gently and expertly. We had not said much to each other, but I felt a warm bond between us. He had pointed out a few things about the plane and answered all my questions, but we had spent most of the trip in a comfortable silence.

When we had come to a stop and the propeller had stopped spinning, I thanked the pilot for such a good flight. He opened the door for me and wished me a "Merry Christmas." I stepped from the plane, feeling like a great actress making the grandest entrance of her life, and there coming across to greet me were the Kanes. Deborah and I raced to each other, squealing with delight. I could tell this was going to be a Christmas to remember.

Next I was loaded into a huge, sleek white convertible car, the flashiest car I had ever seen, with shiny chrome bumpers and not a speck of dirt anywhere. Deborah and I nestled into the soft seats in the back and stared at each other with silly grins on our faces. Mr. and Mrs. Kane looked as perfect as ever, and they beamed at me and asked me how the flight had been. They matched their car for sleekness and polish, and none of them except Deborah seemed quite real to me.

I was bug-eyed with Florida. After being in the Bahamas for nearly four years, I had forgotten how busy and built up and new everything was. We purred by stately rows of towering royal palm trees, past immaculate houses with large, shiny cars parked in their drives. We glided past tall office buildings and stores with beautifully dressed mannequins in their windows. There seemed to be endless stores, with polished plate-glass windows revealing a bright, blurred glimpse of the treasures within. As it was only a week before Christmas, everything was decorated with sparkling tinsel, lush wreathes with huge red bows and pine cones, and gold and silver decorations. The streets were festooned with lights and miles of garlands. All the store fronts were covered in lights and candy canes and plastic reindeer and beaming, waving Santa Clauses. I could only stare and gasp, feeling somewhat dizzy with the trip and the car and all the amazing sights.

It was so different from our preparations for Christmas on

Deep Water Cay, with our small tree and all our handmade decorations. And because Christmas is also Mommy's birthday, Robin and Joel and I had been extra busy making her gifts from shells and other objects we had or could find on the island. Just the thought of my homemade presents made me feel a little embarrassed. What were they compared to all this splendor around me?

When we arrived at the Kane's home, Deborah helped to carry my things up to her bedroom. Their house was grand and luxurious, with high ceilings and white furniture, and a feeling of newness and cleanness. Everything looked as if it had been bought specially just for that house. My favorite house in the whole world was my grandparents' house in Bridgehampton, but that was filled with old furniture, antiques, old paintings, and fading Persian carpets, all bought at other times for other houses. This house was different. It didn't seem to have a past; everything was just exactly the way it appeared. It was almost frighteningly glamorous.

Deborah's bedroom was all that I had ever dreamed of in a bedroom. She had a big pink flouncy bed, some matching furniture, and an impressive array of toys and dolls. I wanted to see everything. I asked her to show me every toy and doll and to tell me their names. Deborah was an only child, and she didn't have any hand-me-downs, nor did she have to share her room or clothes or games or anything. It was all hers and all new. It seemed like heaven.

For most of the time Deborah and I were left to ourselves. We were called down to meals that were prepared by the Kanes' cook. I was slightly shy at mealtimes, and I noticed that no one said grace the way we always did at meals at home. It seemed strange somehow to sit down and start eating immediately. The first few bites felt odd in my mouth, so I said a hurried and silent grace.

We didn't even have to help clear the table or do the dishes. All that was done by servants. Of course, I was used to servants at Deep Water Cay, but I knew we had servants there because of the guests--they were not really our servants. But the Kanes had servants of their own, just for themselves.

I couldn't stop noticing how different Mr. and Mrs. Kane were from my parents, who by comparison looked so much older and dowdier. Mr. Kane was a healthy, bronzed-looking man with dark wavy hair and a movie-star smile. He had big arm muscles and strong legs and not one ounce of a paunch. I couldn't imagine having him as a father. To me, fathers were older and more "worn-in" looking, not bright and bushy-tailed the way he was. But

I liked him and thought him terribly handsome, even though he scared me a little.

Mrs. Kane was the perfect match for her husband. She was the picture of glamour, with smooth, shoulder-length blonde hair and blue eyes. She had a petite figure, and somehow she always gave me the impression of being polished. Even in the clothes she wore when we were not going anywhere special, she looked pristine and unwrinkled--and polished. Like Mr. Kane, she seemed a bit too young for a parent, and she wasn't like my mother who was always hugging and kissing me. Instead she spoke fondly, but rather politely, to Deborah, and rarely gave her spontaneous hugs and kisses. Also she never seemed to get tired or harassed or impatient. She was always cool and calm and in control, and never in a rush, just smooth and uncrumpled.

For the first few days I was in seventh heaven--a friend of my own, in a beautiful house, with hot and cold running everything! There was even a bathtub, and taking a hot bath in the evening was a real treat. All we had in Deep Water Cay was a shower, and most of the time I didn't bother with that, far preferring a swim a day to keep clean. (Until my mother would remark that she couldn't get a brush through my salt-encrusted hair, whereupon I would be made to have a shower and a shampoo.)

But here in Florida with Deborah, I was as shiny and clean and unsalty as she was. I could tell from some of the questions Mr. and Mrs. Kane asked me at dinner that they felt a bit sorry for me. They asked me if I liked living on the island and if I minded not going to a proper school. I didn't understand why they would be sorry for me unless they thought I was lonely. It was hard to explain that even though there were only Robin and Joel and me, most of the time I never felt lonely because there was always so much to do and to think about. I couldn't begin to tell them that if you love shells and you live on a beach, you can never be bored. Even though I was always thrilled to see Deborah and the other children who came to the island from time to time, it was they I felt sorry for when it was time for them to leave, not me.

It also became clear to me that Deborah was not used to having a live-in friend. She was great fun to play with for the first few days, but then she started to behave differently. Sometimes when I would ask to play a certain game, she would make a face and say she didn't want to, but she would not give me a reason why she didn't want to. Sometimes when we were talking she would say she didn't want to talk any more, and she would go off in a state that looked to me a bit like pouting, only I could not understand why on earth she would be pouting. It made me feel awkward and self-conscious. Then I would try to suggest games and other things for us to do, but she would just purse her lips and pout.

This confused and hurt me and made me think of my family back on Deep Water Cay. They would be almost ready for Christmas now, and I could picture my mother racing about, somehow managing to get the lodge to look Christmasy with our few handmade decorations. Before Christmas Robin and Joel and I would collect sand dollars and baby starfish and dry them in the sun. Then we would spray them with gold paint and hang them by threads onto the Christmas tree. The tree was so simple, but I thought it was absolutely beautiful. Now in the Kanes' plush home, even with their tree laden with a selection of valuable, breakable ornaments, I began to miss my family and Deep Water Cay.

On Deep Water Cay if Robin didn't want to play with me, there was Joel; if he didn't want to play with me, there was always the beach to play on, shells to be collected, pictures to be painted, poems to be written, and books to be read. Somehow, here, with Deborah pouting, there didn't seem to be anything else for me to do.

On Christmas Eve I burst into tears. Mrs. Kane must have heard, because she came upstairs to see what the matter was. Deborah had been pouting again, and I had felt so awful, I couldn't stop the tears which had been building up for quite a while. Mrs. Kane tried to make me feel better and scolded Deborah for being unkind, saying that Deborah had to play with me. Of course that only made it worse. It was embarrassing enough to cry in front of Deborah, but it was excruciating to cry in front of her mother. Deborah was behaving like what I know my parents would have called a "spoilt brat," but she was my best friend and had brought me over to stay with her. Her parents were being so generous, and I didn't know what to do!

If only Mommy had been there, she would have known what to do. But Mommy was not there. Mommy was back in Deep Water Cay, getting ready for Christmas, fussing over the guests, and planning surprises for Robin and Joel and Daddy--and no doubt thinking of what a lovely time I was having in Florida. In time I stopped crying, and Deborah and I became friends again.

The next day was Christmas, and nothing could spoil that! Deborah and I woke up early, and whispering and giggling we tiptoed downstairs into the living room. Santa had come all right! What seemed like hundreds of presents lay beneath the tree. Soon Mr. and Mrs. Kane came in, each enveloped in a soft terry-cloth robe, and the unwrapping began.

Deborah handed me a present, her eyes sparkling. It was a

new Barbie doll, complete with a new wardrobe. She was beautiful, and I thought she looked just like Mrs. Kane, only with longer hair. I was given other presents as well, but very soon there were no more presents with my name on them, and there were an awful lot of presents still for Mr. and Mrs. Kane and Deborah!

That Christmas Day was filled with good food and scattered wrapping paper and a happy and excited Deborah. I got to play with all her new toys, and everything felt lovely again, even though it did not feel quite like Christmas. No one read the story of Jesus being born, and we did not go to church or sing any carols. Worst of all, there was no Mommy to sing Happy Birthday to, no Daddy, and no Robin and Joel to compare presents with and play with. It was a wonderful day, but it was not like the Christmases I was used to.

The day after Christmas we were out for a drive when Mr. Kane suddenly pointed to a car going by us and exclaimed, "That was President Kennedy!" I had only seen a big black car go by, but I felt awed to think I had been that close to the President.

It was the next November that President Kennedy was assassinated. We were still in Deep Water Cay, and Daddy heard the news from the BBC's World Service on the ship-to-shore radio. I can remember that I was reading on my bed when Mommy came in, her face tense and her eyes streaming with tears when she told me. At first I did not know what it meant, but slowly I began to realize that our President was dead. Our young, handsome President, whom I had seen driving by in Florida, had been killed.

I had heard of the fate of Abraham Lincoln, so perhaps I supposed it was common for Presidents to be shot. Also, I knew my parents had not voted for Kennedy because he was a Democrat and they were Republicans. Therefore it struck me as odd that Mommy and Daddy were so upset about Kennedy's death. From the things they had said about him in previous conversations which I had overheard, I would have thought they would be pleased to have him out of the way. I did not understand that they could be against some of his policies without actually wanting him dead. They were clearly devastated by his death, and after that I would catch bits of phrases from very serious conversations about the "state of America," and "what our country was coming to," and other dark and gloomy murmurings of which I understood--and wished to understand--nothing.

I don't know what Mr. Kane's job was, but he seemed to have many important looking friends. One man came over to the Kane's house while I was there, and Deborah told me his name in a whisper, assuming I knew who he was. Even though I had never heard his name before, I raised my eyebrows and looked impressed. I didn't dare risk falling out with Deborah again.

But somehow, from Christmas on, I had stopped enjoying my visit. Perhaps the last time Deborah had been pouty with me had started it off, or when I had cried in front of Mrs. Kane. Whatever it was, I had begun to miss my home and family desperately. Once the excitement of Christmas had died away, I could think of nothing else but going home. I knew I only had a few days left in Florida, and I wished they would fly by. I spoke less, and laughed less, and went along with Deborah's games and plans because I did not have the will to create any myself. There was a new and horrible ache inside me, one I had never felt before. It sat above my stomach and it covered my heart and spread up to my throat. It was a dull and draining ache, and it was getting worse and worse. It made me feel physically limp and listless, and at the same time, it gave me an urgent desire to see Mommy and Daddy, to hug and be hugged by them, to feel them and smell their familiar smell.

Then one morning at breakfast, Mrs. Kane smiled at me and said, "Well, girls, you must have a very special day today, because tomorrow Christina goes home." Home. Just the knowledge that I was going home made me bright and cheery again, and I could once again look upon Deborah as a wonderful friend and tell her passionately how much I had loved being with her and how much I would miss her. She was cheery too, and swore how much she would miss me and how she couldn't wait for her parents to go fishing on Deep Water Cay again.

And so I left Deborah, with both of us in high spirits and swearing our affection and loyalty to each other. I flew back on another seaplane, and all I can remember is the rush of the take-off and the plane speeding back over the Gulf Stream, away from the tall buildings, the fancy shops, the tinsel of Christmas, back to Deep Water Cay. I was as tense with excitement as before, but this time it was quite a different type of excitement. I could not wait to get back to what I knew. I had had enough of friends and big houses and beautiful pink bedrooms. I didn't care any more about rows of dolls and closets full of new dresses. All I wanted was my family and to be on Deep Water Cay again.

The skyline of Florida soon turned into a long dark line on the horizon, and we were out over the water, with no land in sight. As we flew, I stared at the horizon ahead and looked down at the wide expanse of sea. I felt as if all the noise and hustle and bustle of what I had left behind was being washed out of me, washed away as I flew. The sound of beeping car horns, the soft rustle of Mrs. Kane gliding across her carpeted floor, the unfamiliar babble of their television, all these sounds grew distant, drowned by the hum of the engine. I became aware of my shoes and how uncomfortable they felt, and I ached to take them off. My dress felt tight and restricting, and I squirmed in it like a trapped animal.

Home. The deep violet became lighter and lighter until we came to the bands of dark blue and aquamarine, the turquoise and light green, and then ahead of us I could make out the lines of Deep Water Cay. We glided down to the water and splashed in gently, once more becoming a large ungainly boat, joining my beloved *Tappan Zee* which was bobbing jauntily at her moorings ahead of us. And there, as we turned the nose of the plane toward the landing strip, there stood the same little group that had waved me off so cheerily only two weeks earlier, waving me home again, welcoming me back to where I belonged.

I hugged Mommy and Daddy as if I would never let go of them, and right there and then I determined never, ever to leave them again.

CHAPTER TWENTY-ONE

The Night the Ceiling Moved

While we lived on Deep Water Cay, we would occasionally take short cruises around other islands in the Bahamas. The waters were perfect for sailing, with many coves and harbors to duck into at night, and long runs between islands. The only bad thing were the reefs, and Daddy and Mommy would pore over their charts to see if we were heading for any particular hazards, such as an old wreck or a large outcropping of coral. Even with up-to-date charts, we could not foresee all the problems. The sands would shift with storms, the reefs would grow, and depending on what the tide was doing, we could be in real danger of running aground.

We did run aground quite a few times, but usually when this happened, with careful maneuvering we could ease ourselves off the bottom and be on our way again. Sometimes it was more serious than that, and Daddy would give a shout that we were all to go up onto the bowsprit in order to weigh down the bow so the stern could be released and swing free. At other times we would lean over one side of the boat, or all go to the stern. When the sea bed was sand, this was a fairly routine procedure, but when we hit coral or rock, Mommy's and Daddy's faces would grow dark as storm clouds, and the atmosphere would be tense and nervous until we were free again.

To prevent going aground, Daddy would take soundings. This was done with a lump of iron (about the size of a large banana) attached to a thin rope, which he would throw out in front of the bow as we moved along. Daddy could tell just how deep the water was from the length of rope that went out before the metal hit bottom. Then he would haul it in furiously and throw it out again and again as we picked our way through a particularly treacherous reef. But mostly the water was deep enough for us to sail or motor gently, enjoying the hot sun and the cool spray and the gorgeous colors around us.

One island we went to was Spanish Wells Island. We had been told that some Spaniards had come to the island years ago and married some of the Bahamians there. Since that time the inhabitants had continued marrying each other until almost everyone on the island was related to one other. My parents said the people had become badly inbred. I didn't really understand what that meant, but as we walked around the island and bought some fresh food at the grocery shop, I began to get some idea.

It was the quietest place I'd ever seen, almost as if everyone were moving in slow motion. Even the children, instead of running around and shouting and playing loudly as usual, were gathered in small groups. Many of them just sat by themselves staring at us as we passed. There were chairs placed outside some of the houses, and in these sat old and not so old people, some blind, some lame, some with vacant expressions, some talking to themselves. There seemed to be a lot of people walking around talking to themselves or just gesticulating as if to an invisible friend. Occasionally some of the people would call out to us a tired greeting or ask a question, sounding too weary to wait for a reply. I clung like a limpet to my mother's side, trying to look friendly but feeling scared inside and very sorry for all the sick and tired and strange-looking people.

We finished our tour of the island and headed back to the dock where we had tied our dinghy. With a sigh of relief we pushed off, and Daddy rowed us out to where the *Tappan Zee* was anchored. Mommy and Daddy were also shaken by what we had seen, and we all talked about the poor inhabitants of Spanish Wells Island for a long time after that. It was as if a sad or cruel or perverted experiment was being lived out on that island, and it looked as if it would continue forever, unless some new blood was introduced. But who would ever want to live there and marry into those families? The place was like a dismal prison, without bars, without a jailor, but a prison just the same.

Once we sailed to an island that was supposedly the site of an ancient place of worship or sacrifice. Evidently there was a huge stone altar somewhere in the interior that hadn't been seen for years and years. Being intrepid explorers, we decided we would search for the altar. We anchored off the island and got dressed in long trousers and long-sleeved shirts; the underbrush seemed so dense from what we could see, we didn't want to get covered in scratches. Daddy took his machete, and we piled into the dinghy and rowed ashore.

The part of the island we had come to was entirely uninhabited, so there were no docks or welcoming committees. Instead, we pulled the dinghy up onto the beach, secured it with a rope around the nearest tree, and set off.

At first it was easy making our way through the bushes and low trees, and we covered a fair distance in good time. But after a while the bushes grew thicker, and the trees became covered in vines which turned the forest into a tangled jungle. Worst of all were the poisonwood trees. A poisonwood tree is a medium-sized tree with a dark brown wood and dark glossy leaves. When the wood of this tree is cut, or even if the leaves are crushed, the sap produces severe welts and a wildly painful and itchy rash.

It seemed now that the entire forest was made up of poisonwood trees, and there was Daddy, hacking his way through them with his machete. There were also spiders, big and brightly marked. Our expedition was turning into a nightmare. But we kept on talking about the altar and how wonderful it would be to find it, and that gave us courage. After a while, however, one by one we started to complain of the itches. I was beginning to feel exhausted and almost dizzy from constant ducking and avoiding branches. Even Daddy began to find the trailblazing hard work.

We had been going for several hours, and even though we all felt sure the altar was right ahead of us, my parents finally made the decision to turn back. We were a dejected and miserable band as we retraced our path, and little whimperings could be heard above the crunching and cracking of our steps. By the time we got back to the beach, we were all on fire, especially Daddy. He had been covered in poisonwood sap and his skin was erupting in angry welts and blotches. Besides that, we had to shake out our clothes before we boarded the *Tappan Zee*, because we had collected collars and sleeves full of leaves, and bits of branch, and insects.

It had been a difficult and creepy trek, and all for nothing. Back on board we covered ourselves with calamine lotion, which helped to take away the stinging. Yet despite our failure to find the altar, I had found it an exciting trip. It had made me feel tough and strong and fearless, and long after that I used to imagine what it would have been like if we had found the altar, and how we could have made a large clearing and built a house there and been genuine explorers. What if there had been another altar, or maybe some ancient artifacts, or most exciting of all, what if we had discovered some prehistoric people still living on the deserted island? As we sailed away from the shores of the mysterious island, itching madly, my imagination was as active and on fire as my rashes, and all I could think about was going back one day and not giving up.

Going to Spanish Wells and the poisonwood island had been fascinating adventures, but the greatest adventure of all on strange islands was still to come. One gloriously clear morning, a friend of my parents named Jim came to see us with a wonderful proposition; he invited us all to come out in his motorboat for a whole day's trip. Daddy was busy repairing some motors or boats, and he could not get away, but to our delight, Mommy agreed to come out for the day. We waved goodbye to Daddy and piled aboard Jim's small, fast motorboat.

The sun was sparkling on the water, and we were in high spirits. The breeze blew warm air over our faces and through our hair. The boat bounced over the small waves, with the engine making a comforting hum. We decided to head for a group of virtually unknown islands. Jim had calculated that it would take nearly half the day to reach them, then we could spend a few hours exploring, and be back by nightfall. We settled down for a long, sunny trip.

By the early afternoon the wind had come up a bit. Instead of prancing merrily over the waves, we had begun to bash into them head on. Along the horizon behind us, there was a strip of clouds that seemed to be following us to the island. Mommy and Jim discussed turning back, but we were now closer to the islands than home. So we sped on, scrunching up our faces against the spray. The wind blew harder, and the motion of the boat became more violent. This was not at all like the pleasure trip it was supposed to be.

The clouds behind us were gaining on us and had grown large and dark. It was turning into a squall. A squall is a special type of storm over sea that can happen almost without warning. One minute there is clear sky, the next a howling gale. There are degrees of squalls which all sea dwellers can recognize. The worst is the white squall, so called because the sky turns an ominous pale gray before it pours with rain and lashes with ferocious winds. Our beautiful day was turning into an angry stormy blast. We reckoned we were being overtaken by a white squall, and we were anxious to get to the island and find some shelter.

When we finally reached the island, the seas were wild, and the storm was nearly upon us. Jim steered the boat right up onto the beach, and we all hopped out and helped him pull the boat further up the sand. Jim tied a rope from the boat around a palm tree, and we scuttled up the beach.

Our approach had not gone unnoticed. As we went running inland, we were met by a group of about fifty people of all ages. We later discovered it was the entire population of the island. Children hid behind their mothers' blowing skirts and peeped out at us with huge eyes. A small group of children led by an adult started singing a song for us. I was uncomfortable with the attention we were receiving but very curious as well. A spokesman for the group welcomed us in a grand and formal way. It was a strange gathering, with us in our boating gear and blown hair, and the islanders in their patched clothing and bare feet.

My mother bent down and whispered to us, "Smile and don't stare. They have never seen white people before. We are the first to come." This was very exciting and we stared even harder! We may have tried to smile, but we were too shy and hungry to manage much more than a wobbly grimace apiece.

Then the squall broke upon us. The rain swept down in sheets and the wind bent the palm trees low. There was immediate bedlam. The people scattered, shouting and calling and screaming. We were ushered swiftly into a small house nearby. It seemed that half the village crammed in after us. We were packed into one room while the owner of the house started to light some oil lamps. There was laughter and loud talking, a party atmosphere. Robin and Joel and I stood in a damp huddle, feeling tired and hungry, and looking exceedingly bedraggled, while Mommy spoke to the host.

When Mommy came back, she informed us we would be spending the night in the house. We may have then been given something to eat, but I have no recollection of any meal. All I remember is going into another room and stripping off my wet clothes and climbing into a small bed with Robin, head to feet. Joel was tucked up in another bed in the same room, where he would be joined later by Mommy. Evidently, Jim had been invited to sleep in another house. Mommy kissed us goodnight, and I fell asleep to the sound of laughter and talking, muffled by the sound of the wind and the rain.

Suddenly, hours later, I was awakened by my mother's voice, urgent and tense: "What was that? Joel! What was that?" Robin and I were fully awake, sitting up and blinking in the dark. Then we heard Joel whisper in a wobbly voice, "Mommy, the ceiling is moving." We all looked up at the ceiling. There was just enough light shining through from the other room for us to make out strange shifting patterns on the ceiling, like rain blowing in waves, making pitter-patter sounds. Joel said sleepily, "It's raining on the ceiling." Something was wrong. How could rain fall on the inside of a roof? And if it did, why did it not fall down on us?

Just then Mommy screamed and jumped out of bed. "There's something on my pillow," she panted. "It's right beside me!" Joel had shot under the covers, and Robin and I each grabbed our end of the sheet and pulled it over our heads. Mommy told us to stay underneath our covers. She made her way across the dark room and opened the door a crack into the other room. We could hear her asking if she could borrow a lamp. Her voice sounded brittle. A few seconds later she stepped back into our room, followed by an old lady holding a lamp. We peered out from under the covers and looked up to see the dark pitter-patter shapes on the ceiling divide like a sea parting and melt into the black corners. The rain was not rain. Up on the ceiling and now disappearing into the darkness were hundreds, perhaps thousands, of huge cockroaches and even larger spiders. They had been engaged in a battle royal right above our heads. On the floor beside Mommy's bed we could see the retreating forms of a fallen cockroach being dragged away by a monstrous spider. We all screamed and dived under our covers again.

Mommy tried to speak in a controlled voice, politely, even delicately. "The spiders . . . Uh . . . the roaches . . . uh . . . ?" Her voice trailed off, and she swallowed hard. The old woman grinned and giggled. "They all right," she chirped. "They don't hurt you. If theys fall on you, jest flick 'em off." She flicked my mother's shoulder cheerily by way of a demonstration. Mommy nodded, mute, then asked, "Could we keep the lamp for a while?" "Why sho', sho'," the woman beamed, and plunked the lamp on a table. She turned to go back into the other room where there were still voices, then added with another giggle, "Jest flick 'em off, flick 'em off!" The moment the door was closed, my mother jumped back into bed next to Joel. "The light will keep them away," she whispered, "but keep your sheets over your heads." We did not need to be told. Stuffy though it was, all of us hid beneath our bedclothes for the rest of the night.

In the morning, we rose, dressed, and met up with Jim, who said we could make it home. Even though the storm had died down, the sea was still blustery--but luckily, navigable. We said our thank yous and goodbyes and pushed off from the beach.

Daddy was as delighted to see us safe and sound as we were delighted to see him again. We told and retold the events of that night to each other, reliving the horror in the safe light of the day. We reckoned that the cockroaches had been over two inches long and the spiders even larger, including legs. None of us had ever seen such large specimens before, and we had no idea what type of roaches or spiders they were. Even now, the memory of that night sends shivers down my spine. I call it the night the ceiling moved.

CHAPTER TWENTY-TWO

Chased by Sharks

While living at Deep Water Cay, we made several trips to other islands. During one of these trips we sailed to a small remote place called Berry Island where we anchored off a deserted palm-fringed beach.

It was midmorning and we could not wait to get into the water. Besides, we wanted some fish for lunch. We had the whole day to explore the coral reefs around us. My father took the spear gun and swam off with Robin in search of lunch. Mommy and Joel paddled off together, and I went off with our Aunt Ogi who was staying with us for about a month.

We swam in pairs as a precaution. In swimming and diving, there is too much that can go wrong, and divers all over the world abide by this rule. We were not scuba diving, but even in shallow water there were dangers of which we had to be aware. Sometimes one's equipment can create problems; for instance a leaky mask or snorkel may flood unexpectedly. Severe cramps can debilitate even the strongest swimmer. Also, two pairs of eyes are better than one. It is best to swim with a friend in case of an attack from a fish or some other danger.

The waters of the Bahamas were infested with sharks. Even though many of the varieties were the smaller sharks, they were sharks nonetheless. Occasionally one of the guests would catch a shark off Deep Water Cay, and the guide would slit open its stomach to see what it had eaten for its last meal. More than once, human remains were found, and I remember seeing one particularly ghoulish discovery, a human finger. We had swum with sharks on many occasions. We were becoming so accustomed to them that if they stayed in the distance and did not display any interest in us, then we usually kept on swimming. But if they headed toward us or seemed excited in any way, we got out of the water, just to be on the safe side.

Much has been written about sharks and many stories told,

but there is still a lot we do not know about them. Their size and strength make them frightening, and the sight of a black fin slicing through the water at speed is enough to chill even the most experienced swimmer. To me, sharks were the ultimate threat. There was something about their blunt, bullet-shaped heads, their rows of wicked-looking teeth, and their large cold eyes that kept sharks at the top of my list of things most hated and most feared. Ogi and I set off side by side, pointing out to each other the tiny bright, darting fish, the coral, and the swaying sea fans and anemones. We had on masks, flippers, and snorkels, so we could glide quietly while surveying the beautiful world just a few feet beneath us.

Ogi and I spotted a sun fish that day, which was very exciting because it was so rare. A sun fish looks like the head of an ordinary fish, just a large swimming head without a body. We were thrilled and made big eyes at each other from within our masks. The reef was full of color and life, and we forgot time as we wended our way slowly over the coral.

At one point Ogi and I looked straight down, and there, six feet below us, was a shark resting on the sandy bottom, half hidden by an overhanging ledge of coral. We froze in terror, but the shark just looked back up at us with its dark eyes, without moving. There was absolutely nothing we could have done to escape had the shark attacked us. We stared at each other for a while, and then Ogi and I swam on, glancing back from time to time to make sure the shark was not following us. It did not stir.

We were still lazily floating over the reef when all of a sudden we heard a yell. We stuck our heads up out of the water and tried to see who had called out. I saw Mommy and Joel, heads also up, about fifty feet away from us. Much further out, Daddy and Robin were waving and shouting. Ogi and I could not make out what they were saying, but the message was unmistakably clear: "HEAD FOR THE BEACH!"

We turned instantly, and I swam toward the shore as hard and fast as I have ever swum. Ogi and I reached the beach first and scrambled out, flippers and all. Mommy and Joel were only seconds behind us, panting and gasping for breath. Then Daddy and Robin made the beach, splashing frantically as they clambered out of the shallow water.

And then we saw them. It was a sight which froze us solid. Hard on the heels of Daddy and Robin were about a dozen speeding black shapes and shiny black dorsal fins. Sharks!

Daddy and Robin hurled themselves up on the sand, inches ahead of their attackers. The sharks were swimming so quickly that they came shooting up on the beach, their noses burrowing in the sand, their jaws open and snapping. The whole scene was charged with a sense of manic bloodthirstiness. Then the sharks, realizing they were out of the water, flipped and writhed wildly, desperately trying to shimmy themselves back into the sea. After they had wriggled themselves back into the water, the sharks circled swiftly and erratically for a while. Then suddenly, without warning, they vanished into deeper water.

The six of us lay on the beach, covered with sand, unable to move or speak. We stared at the water which was once again lapping innocently on the sand. Then we all started talking at once. "Did you see them!" "They came out of nowhere!" "I didn't see them coming."

"They were after the grouper." My father had the explanation. He had speared a large grouper, a fleshy and delicious-tasting fish. The grouper had swum into a coral crevasse with the spear still in its side, bleeding profusely. Daddy had tried to get at the grouper, but it backed further into the small cave, its blood spreading around it in the water.

The next thing Daddy remembers is seeing a shark far in the distance swimming toward them. That was when he and Robin had yelled for the rest of us to get out of the water. Then they had started swimming madly for the shore, little realizing that the one shark had been joined by others. Sharks have an acute sense of smell and can detect minute amounts of blood in the water. The death throes of the grouper had served as an excellent invitation to lunch. It was a miracle that the rest of us had heard Robin's and Daddy's shouts and that we had responded instantly. None of us had wasted the time to call back to them, "Why, what is it?" or "What's the matter?"

We could understand how Ogi and I, and even Mommy and Joel, had gotten safely to the shore, but we have never understood how Daddy and Robin made it. Even though they had a good head start, they should not have been able to outswim the sharks. We figured there must have been so much splashing and confusion in the shallow water that the sharks had not been able to focus clearly on Robin and Daddy. But truth to tell, even with this plausible explanation, we all felt it was a miracle. We lay on the beach for a long time, panting, talking, crying. And we said a prayer of thanks to God.

We waited on the beach until we could all get up and face going back into the water. We had to return to the *Tappan Zee* which was anchored quite a way off shore. We swam together in a close group. That swim took all our collective courage, but we did it. Daddy never recovered his spear, and we did not have fish for lunch.

After a while we could laugh about the sharks and make fun of them, so intent on getting us that they had beached themselves! We would wriggle from side to side, the way the sharks had done to get back into the water, and we mocked their frenzied attack. That was the closest call we ever had with sharks, at least that we knew about. We all felt God had stepped in that day, and helped us out--in the nick of time!

CHAPTER TWENTY-THREE

The Storm

During our time at sea we sailed through innumerable squalls and storms. We had to outmaneuver the sea tornadoes that sped over the surface of the sea, sucking water up into their huge elongated cones, only to deposit it elsewhere with violence. We weathered at least five hurricanes, and I grew to know their pattern. First, there is a fierce wind in one direction, followed by an eerie calm which lasts for about an hour, and then a fierce wind blowing in the opposite direction. Even though we had had our mast broken in a freak tornado and our sails torn in various storms, we had always managed to maintain the sense, if not the reality, of being in control. I had an absolute trust in Mommy and Daddy. If they were with me nothing too desperate could happen. The fiendish powers of the sea and winds might be able to gobble up a small child, but certainly not while its parents were around. So I kept the furies at bay with my confidence in my parents. Sometimes the elements snarled loudly and bared their teeth, but I could always turn my back on them if I stayed close to Mommy and Daddy.

Life on board the *Tappan Zee* was a life of constant risk. When we had begun our voyage, years earlier, Joel had fallen overboard almost daily. In time, however, his balance and sense of self-preservation improved, and Robin and I did not have to cry out so often, "Mommy, Daddy, come quickly! Joel's fallen overboard!"

It was possible for anything and everything to go wrong. Every time we tied up to a new mooring, there was the potentially hazardous jump from boat to shore. In some places it required swinging oneself from the rigging and hurling oneself onto land. And to come back on board, there were times when we had to take running leaps and hope we would be able to grab a rope or a bit of the rigging or Daddy's outstretched hand. Usually we made it, but there were times when we, or the things we were carrying, missed and fell into the water. There was very little leeway for hesitation or timidity, and there were many times when I jumped simply because I had to.

We operated as a team during the traditionally critical moments, when coming into a harbor in rough seas or when in a storm. Daddy, as captain, would bark out orders to hold a rope, or pull, or fend us off a dock. I learned to hold a rope even when it threatened to slip out of my hands. I learned to brace myself against something immovable and hold on with every ounce of strength I possessed. Sometimes, when the crisis was over, we would have to nurse rope burns across the palms of our hands or splinters embedded deep in our flesh. Our muscles grew strong and hard, our balance became excellent, as well as our ability to put up with hours and days of heavy seas or relentless winds. I could be shivering with cold and still pull up a sail, or nearly passing out in the heat, and carry on steering the boat. I knew the feeling of intense thirst and hunger and the feeling of salt coating my hair and skin. There were times when we slept fully dressed and times when I was so tired I could not even take off my shoes before collapsing into my bunk. During heavy rains our entire boat would be drenched, and there were the times when we had to sleep in damp clothes on a damp mattress covered with damp bedding. There was no escape.

I overcame many of the petty, squeamish dislikes I had started out with, but I did not conquer all my fears on the boat; in fact, some grew worse. Unfortunately the fear of lightning and sharks did not diminish with familiarity. However, I did learn that I could usually do more than I thought I could, and that if Mommy or Daddy said, "Do it!" then I could, even if sometimes I did it with tears running down my face and clenched teeth, while screaming back at them, "I can't. I can't!"

Our entire family was always covered with bruises. We were constantly bumping ourselves or being hit by something. Our bodies were firm, and we were all uncommonly strong and agile. Because I usually ran around barefoot, the skin on the bottom of my feet grew thick and hard. Once, for fun, I threaded a needle with some colored thread and sewed flowery patterns through the top few layers of skin on the soles of my feet. I thought it was rather pretty, but Mommy thought it was disgusting and forbade me from doing it again. To me it was natural; I had absolutely no idea I was different from any other ten-year-old American girl.

Toward the end of our time in the Bahamas, we were caught in the tail of a wild hurricane. We were in the process of returning to Deep Water Cay after one of our sailing excursions and were only about half a day away. But the wind came up and we had nowhere to go. There was not even place for us to anchor. We were sailing over treacherous reefs which sometimes came up to the surface of the water. If we had tried to find shelter near an island, we could have ripped the bottom off our boat. The only thing for us to do was head for deeper water and hope that the wind would soon die down.

All that day we pushed on into the storm. We took everything that was not tied down on deck, below, so it would not be washed overboard. We children put on our life jackets, and the time came when Mommy and Daddy put theirs on too. We tried to reorganize some of the loose objects below. With every wave, plates would rattle, books would slide, and tins would roll in their cupboards. Robin and Joel and I did the best we could while being thrown around ourselves.

Rather than letting up, the storm grew worse. By sundown we had adopted a siege mentality. All thoughts of getting back to Deep Water Cay that day, even eating supper or getting to sleep that night, evaporated. We thought only of surviving the storm.

The seas became more wild, and the waves loomed like dark mountains on either side of us. Daddy struggled to steer the boat while Mommy peered into the storm attempting to determine the best way for us to take each wave. She was gripping the boom tightly as she stood, barely able to see and barely able to stand. All of a sudden the boom ripped from its cradle and swung wildly out over the water with Mommy still hanging on. Mommy held on for dear life until the boat leaned to the other side and she came swinging back. Daddy grabbed the boom as it went by, and Mommy dropped off on the deck. Together they struggled to secure the boom again, no small feat at any time, but now, nearly impossible with their being pitched about in the gloom. The boom was a solid tree trunk, stretching about twenty feet in length, with a diameter of four and a half inches, not an easy object to handle. After that, Mommy tied one end of a rope around her waist and fastened the other end to a cleat on the deck.

Then the next disaster struck. Mommy and Daddy heard a loud bang from somewhere in the rigging, but they could not see what had happened. Daddy looked at the masts to see if one of them had broken. He tugged at the various wires of the rigging to see if they had broken. Finally he discovered what had happened. Underneath the bowsprit the front end of one of the rigging wires had broken off. It was the bobstay, the thick wire that stretches up and across both mast tops and down again to keep the masts in their proper tension. With a bobstay broken, a sailboat runs the risk of having its masts come loose and all the other rigging collapse. It is one of the most vital pieces of a sailboat. Daddy staggered back from the bow and shouted the bad news. Then he came down below to collect the tools he would need to repair it. It was not a question of waiting to see if it would be all right. He knew he had to fix it immediately.

Down below, the jerking and swaying motion had gotten too

much for us. Robin and Joel and I were all sick, repeatedly. We found two buckets and held on to them in the dark, two of us hunched over one. Every time the boat heeled to one side, we would be thrown against that side of the boat. And then with the next wave, we would be thrown across the cabin to the other side. We retched with each wave.

Daddy found the necessary tools and tied them onto a piece of rope which he then tied around his waist. We could tell that whatever had happened was serious and that we were in trouble. At one point I could not stand the stench of my own vomit any longer; also I was desperate to see if Mommy and Daddy were all right. I climbed the ladder and pushed back the hatch cover. Immediately I was drenched with water. Mommy screamed at me from her position at the tiller, "Get down! Don't open the hatch!"

I slammed the hatch cover shut and was thrown down the stairs. It was worse on deck than I had thought. Daddy made his way up to the bow again and lashed himself to the forward mast. Then he lay down over the bowsprit and fumbled for the ripped wire.

The waves were hitting us sideways, and we were in danger of being capsized. Because it was dark, Mommy could not see well enough to judge how to take each wave. The best way would have been to head into the waves, but it was difficult to turn the boat against the power of the wind and the force of the waves. Mommy finally managed to head us more into the storm. Now with every wave, we rose up and up until we came crashing down in the trough, the boat groaning and shuddering in agony.

Every time we went up, Daddy worked frantically. Then when he could feel the boat falling again, he held tightly to the bowsprit and took a deep breath. As we sank into each trough, Daddy was plunged under water until the boat rose with the next wave. This rising and plunging lasted throughout the night, with Mommy gauging the best way to take each wave, and Daddy forcing his numbed hands to mend the bobstay in the pitch dark. The three of us children were still being thrown back and forth across the cabin. We had become too weak even to hold onto our buckets any longer and we threw up all over our clothes, all over the cabin, now nothing but acrid bile left in our stomachs.

This went on and on, and I vaguely remember whispering in my head, "Please God, don't let us die." I think we were all praying that silent prayer, and that night God heard us and was merciful.

At last Daddy refastened the bobstay. It had taken him several endless hours, and he had risked his life to do it. The boat now had a chance. Mommy noticed she could see the waves more clearly, now that they were outlined against a bruised dawn sky. We had made it through the night!

As the sky lightened, the waves became less fierce. Robin and Joel and I finally stopped getting thrown across the cabin. We lay hunched on the bunks in the main cabin, limp with fatigue, seasickness, and the strain of trying to brace ourselves against the pitching of the waves. It was raining and the wind was still blowing, but the crisis was over. It was as if we had been blinded by the night so we did not have to look the storm in the eye. Perhaps God knew we would make it, as long as we did not have to see it as well.

Daddy now sat with Mommy at the tiller. Both of them were sodden and exhausted from the battle. The sun finally cleared the ragged horizon and the seas died to a steady swell. There, in the distance, we could make out the line of Deep Water Cay! We were closer than we thought. We limped home saying little, too tired to speak, not quite believing we had made it. We tied up to our familiar dock under a gray weeping sky and walked weakly and unsteadily back up to the lodge--and slept.

We did not return to the *Tappan Zee* until that evening. We were all like wrung-out rags. When we did go back to the boat, Mommy was the first to push open the hatch. She saw the moon reflected on the floor of the cabin, where it was not supposed to be. There was about an inch of water covering the floor. The boat was slowly filling with water. Daddy pulled the boat around to the side of the dock so it would come to rest on the sand when the tide went out. And then we all went back to bed.

In the morning we came down to find the *Tappan Zee* high and dry on the sand, tilted on her side like a beached whale. Daddy inspected the sides and bottom carefully, and he found several seams which had come loose in the storm. The boat had been pounded nearly to death by the ferocious unrelenting waves. During the following week, Daddy re-caulked and tightened the seams, and the *Tappan Zee* was soon returned to the water, shipshape and watertight once again.

Later, we all compared stories of that night and heard how each of us had fared. What Mommy had not told us was that during the worst of the night, the waves had been over twenty feet high. She could guess the height by how far back she had had to crane her neck to make out the tops of the waves. She remembered staring up and up to see a mountain of water either beside us or in front of us. Daddy too reckoned they were over twenty feet high. No wonder he had been plunged under water with every wave.

We accepted that living on a boat meant facing potential life and death situations, but we all sensed how close we had come to death that night. If the storm had gone on for much longer, the boat would have probably broken up and sunk. That had been clear when we discovered the water over the floor boards.

True, we could have died from our encounter with the sharks off Berry Island, and no doubt at other places that we may not even have been aware of, but the night of the storm was different. I think what set it apart was that we had actually had to fight hard for our lives through an entire night. It has helped me understand a little of what people must go through when they live in fear, not only for hours, as we did, but for a lifetime. That one night was enough for me.

Epilogue

We left Deep Water Cay and the Bahamas in the summer of 1964, and sailed back across the Gulf Stream to Florida. There we left the boat and drove up to Long Island. Grandpapa was ill, and we decided to stay with him and help in the big house. While we were at Deep Water Cay, both of Mommy's parents had died. She had flown all the way to California to her mother's funeral, but when a little while later her father died, she stayed on the island and wept.

Mommy and Daddy let us keep our shell collections, and for days before we left Deep Water Cay, we carefully wrapped the best of our shells in newspaper and toilet paper, snuggling them into cardboard and wooden boxes. That was one of the most generous things they could have done, because we each had about five boxes apiece--except for Daddy who had not collected many shells. Besides the shells, we had coral, starfish, turtle shells, sea fans, and many other treasures. At the final count, over twenty boxes were shipped to New York.

Leaving Deep Water Cay was heart-wrenching. The ladies and the guides did not want us to go. I can still see the sad group of friends standing on the dock waving to us. Most of them, even the men, had tears streaming down their faces as we sailed away. And so did we.

We crossed the Gulf Stream, admiring once again the brilliant clarity of the water, but this time Mommy made the porridge with fresh water! We intended to stay on Long Island for the summer and then return to the boat and Florida and a new adventure. But in November, Grandpapa died. Daddy spent a year making an inventory of the estate which was to be divided between Daddy and his sisters and brother. My parents decided to buy the house.

Mommy put us in the local school where we found ourselves ahead in most subjects. We were all somewhat homesick for Deep Water Cay. We children had developed a strange accent, a mixture of British and Bahamian, and the other children found us exotic. Being different was a mixed blessing. At times we were begged for stories about life on the boat, and at other times we were accused of boasting about our past. Life among our peer groups was new territory for us, and it felt as uncomfortable as sailing through a gale.

It was two years before we went to live on the boat again. My parents had planned a year of sailing around the Mediterranean. They figured we only had about one year left as a family before Robin would have to study for university exams. We decided not to take the three months it would require to sail across the Atlantic, so we had the *Tappan Zee* shipped to Savona, a small Italian town just north of Genoa.

That was an amazing year with tales of its own. I met a golden god named Alexis who tried to seduce me underwater in the same bay from which Ulysses had sailed. And there was the day in the harbor near Rome when Daddy broke a rib and ankle and nearly drowned, all because Joel had gone to get me some grapes. There was Christmas when the police broke into a bakery shop to get a cake for Mommy, and the times when we were almost blown up in Naples and almost shipwrecked in Greece.

We sailed into Rhodes on the morning of my fourteenth birthday. I remember taking a night watch all by myself, trimming the sails and watching the compass, sailing through the night, the only one awake. That was a night of glory. But, as they say, these are stories for another time.

I still have my shells and starfish and sea fans, and if I miss anything in life, I miss the feeling of diving into my underwater world where all is silence and beauty and where the fish dance in front of my mask and the crawfish challenge me to a duel and I become weightless and grow fins and frolic with the porpoises and mermaids. No matter how grown-up I become or how far from the sea I live, I will never be able to wash the soft sand off my feet or the salt water out of my hair. And there are days when, if I listen hard, there is a child in me who is calling me out to play on a long white beach rimmed with sea oats and sea grape trees where the skies are blue and the seas are warm and the days go on forever. "I shall come," I promise the child. "One day I shall come."